Joseph Tuthill Duryea

Selections from the Psalms and Other Scriptures

In the Revised Version for Responsive Reading in Church Services and on Special

Occasions

Joseph Tuthill Duryea

Selections from the Psalms and Other Scriptures
In the Revised Version for Responsive Reading in Church Services and on Special Occasions

ISBN/EAN: 9783337020835

Printed in Europe, USA, Canada, Australia, Japan

Cover: Foto ©Lupo / pixelio.de

More available books at **www.hansebooks.com**

SELECTIONS

FROM

THE PSALMS AND OTHER SCRIPTURES

IN THE

REVISED VERSION,

FOR

RESPONSIVE READING IN CHURCH SERVICES AND ON
SPECIAL OCCASIONS.

EDITED BY

REV. JOSEPH T. DURYEA, D.D.

BOSTON AND CHICAGO:
Congregational Sunday-School and Publishing Society.

PREFACE.

The following pages contain portions of the Sacred Scriptures selected chiefly from the Psalms, but also from the Prophets, the Gospels, the Epistles, and the Revelation, for the use of Christian congregations in public worship. The most of them are appropriate to the ordinary services of the Lord's Day. The rest are adapted to the special services of Christmas, Easter, Thanksgiving Day, Fast Day, missionary meetings, and the Lord's Supper.

These selections are not designed to be read with the aim of instruction, but to be recited for the ends of worship. The book is not a lectionary, but a manual of devotion.

In the view of the writers, both of the Old Testament and the New, worship[1] is the offering to God of thought and emotion in some form of expression. The worshiper is not passive, but active; not the subject of impressions, but the agent of expressions. It is enough that his mind be engaged in thought, his heart excited to emotion. He must "direct," "lift up," his soul to God, and signify or utter his sentiment, his thoughtful emotion, to him.

This is clear enough with respect to those exercises which all agree in recognizing as acts of worship. These are all directed to God and expressive. Otherwise they are not complete, however proper and salutary they may be to the spiritual life. Contemplation of the majesty and perfection of God with emotions of reverence and admiration is not *adoration;* recollection of the divine mercies with the emotion of gratitude is not *thanksgiving;* consideration of dependence and need with the feeling of desire is not *prayer.* If the familiar lines,

"Prayer is the soul's sincere desire,
Uttered or unexpressed,"

be interpreted in the strict sense of the words and taken as a true description for guidance in practice, the result will be perilous, if not

---

[1] The Greek word denotes an act of reverence, whether paid to man (see chap. 18: 26) or to God (see chap. 4: 10). *Note IV of the American Committee to Revised Version.*

fatal, to that life which is quickened and sustained by communion with God. The poet is in error, unless by "uttered" he means *spoken*, and by "unexpressed," *unspoken*. Desire may be signified, and so become supplication or petition, by other tokens than those of articulate speech, as the poet himself says in his stanzas following. But, still, speech is the natural medium of devotion. Our Lord, when asked to teach his disciples how to pray, responded: "When ye pray, say, Our Father," etc. The apostle teaches, "In everything, by prayer and supplication, with thanksgiving, let your requests be made known unto God." He who is revealed in the High-priest, who "can be touched with the feeling of our infirmities," no doubt regards the "burden of a sigh," and the "falling of a tear,"—so he does the fall of a sparrow, but it is not a prayer.

From the earliest ages, among all races which have cherished the religious sentiments, song has been a natural, though not universal, means of expression in worship. The poet has framed the language of emotion in the lyrical form, and the musician has adapted to it fit melodies, sung often with the accompaniment of instruments.

These hymns have been, for the most part, devotional, not indirectly, but directly so, addressed to God. The call to sing them might appropriately have been that which was so familiar to the Hebrew people, "O come let us sing *unto the Lord!*" Among their own psalms, preserved to us, by far the greater number were utterances of penitence, confession, aspiration, thanksgiving, petition, faith, hope, love to God. Though sung by sentences alternately, or, as we say, "responsively," or "antiphonally," they were sung in the spirit of the apostle's exhortation, "speaking to one another in psalms and hymns and spiritual songs, singing and making melody in your hearts unto the Lord." [1]

There are, indeed, psalms in which the patriotic blends with the religious sentiments, and even such as the worshipers were wont to address to each other, designed to excite the emotions and incite to noble action in the service of Jehovah. But these simply make it evident that song has no religious uses aside from the ends of pure worship. But even these battle-songs and triumphal anthems were sung as in the presence of Jehovah, in the spirit of another exhortation of the same apostle, "teaching and admonishing one another in

[1] Ephesians 5: 19.

psalms and hymns and spiritual songs, singing with grace in your hearts unto the Lord."[1]

Song, then, has been a natural, though not universal, means of devotional expression; not universal inasmuch as all men are not endowed with musical gifts, bodily and mental. Speech alone is general and nearly universal, and must be always the common medium of worship.

If it be asked whether the deaf and dumb, the feeble, the paralyzed, and the dying, can not acceptably worship, and, especially, "make their prayer unto God," the answer is plain. It is not to be doubted that they may direct their souls to God, and so seek him as to find him, so ask as to receive. But they can not present those offerings of worship which we are taught in the Scriptures to offer to God. Men, from any cause defective, can not perform perfect acts, though their intention is accepted. The will is taken for the deed.

There can be no question, however, concerning the manner of common worship. Without some form of expression it can not be the united offering of the worshipers. It is true there may be a leader of devotions, whose utterances the people may understand and adopt. But this implies all we have affirmed, though not completely. It would be better if the custom of the Christian assemblies of apostolic times were followed, the people saying, Amen, at the pauses, or at the close of the prayer. It is one of the lasting excellencies of a liturgy that it provides for utterances from the people in unison, and, accordingly, in "decency and in order."

This exposition of the Scriptural conception of worship is designed to encourage the adoption of such methods in our religious services as may engage the entire congregation in acts of devotion, directed immediately to God, expressive of thought and emotion to him. It is also intended to meet the objection made by respectable authorities that such selections as these here presented are essentially, and most of them formally, lyrical, and, accordingly, proper to be sung and not to be read. Indeed, it has recently been asserted that it is quite absurd to read them as we commonly do, that the correct thing is to have them sung antiphonally by different choirs, in case of the Psalms, which consist of parallel phrases reiterating the sentiment, and, in case of the Doxologies, in full chorus. This, no doubt, might

[1] Colossians 3: 16.

be best if all congregations were composed of singers, and all the singers were trained to the task.

At present, in many congregations, the services are such as make no call and afford no help to the people to engage in acts of worship. Prayer is made for them or on their behalf; praise is sung for them, this too often nominally, while, in fact, music is performed for æsthetic effect — is not spiritual or even religious in design and tone; and preaching is addressed to them. In the churches in which the people speak audibly in prayer, and so many as are able sing in praise, the recitation of the Psalms affords an opportunity for expression to those who have neither the voice nor the musical ear for song. It is for this purpose that these selections have been prepared. By way of emphasis, it is repeated, they are not intended to be read as lessons. For each of them the rubric of the Canticles in the prayer-book would be gladly adopted " to be SAID or sung."

The division into phrases for alternate recitation by the minister and the people has been made with care, and, as far as practicable, is natural, according to the movement of the sentiment. In many instances the parallelisms of the original have been followed. Where the phrases are short they have been neglected, since experience has shown that otherwise there can not be such rhythm and flow in the recitation as are needful to the best effect. In this departure pains have been taken to secure congruity and symmetry in the alternate parts.

The Revised Version has been used for the reason that it is a more exact expression of the original text. Such use of it as is here contemplated may incidentally furnish a test to a common objection to the Revised Version, namely, that its style is not rhythmical and fluent, and, therefore, resonant and impressive in the utterance.

JOSEPH T. DURYEA.

NOTE.

The following selections are arranged to be read by the Minister and the People responsively, according to their original structure and design.

The lines printed in Roman letters are to be read by the Minister.

The lines set inward from the margin, and printed in Black letters, are to be read by the People.

The lines printed in small capitals are to be read by the Minister and the People together.

RESPONSIVE READINGS.

PSALM I.

Blessed is the man that walketh not in the counsel of the wicked,
　Nor standeth in the way of sinners,
　Nor sitteth in the seat of the scornful.
But his delight is in the law of the Lord;
　And in his law doth he meditate day and night.
And he shall be like a tree planted by the streams of water,
　That bringeth forth its fruit in its season,
Whose leaf also doth not wither;
　And whatsoever he doeth shall prosper.
The wicked are not so; but are like the chaff which the wind driveth away.
　Therefore the wicked shall not stand in the judgment, nor sinners in the congregation of the righteous.
For the Lord knoweth the way of the righteous:
　But the way of the wicked shall perish.

PSALM II.

Why do the nations rage,
　And the peoples imagine a vain thing?
The kings of the earth set themselves,
　And the rulers take counsel together,
　Against the Lord, and against his anointed, saying,

Let us break their bands asunder,
  And cast away their cords from us.
He that sitteth in the heavens shall laugh:
  The Lord shall have them in derision.
Then shall he speak unto them in his wrath,
  And vex them in his sore displeasure:
Yet I have set my king
Upon my holy hill of Zion.
  I will tell of the decree:
  The Lord said unto me, Thou art my son;
  This day have I begotten thee.
Ask of me, and I will give thee the nations for thine inheritance,
  And the uttermost parts of the earth for thy possession.
Thou shalt break them with a rod of iron;
  Thou shalt dash them in pieces like a potter's vessel.
Now therefore be wise, O ye kings:
  Be instructed, ye judges of the earth.
Serve the Lord with fear,
And rejoice with trembling.
  Kiss the son, lest he be angry, and ye perish in the way,
  For his wrath will soon be kindled.
BLESSED ARE ALL THEY THAT PUT THEIR TRUST IN HIM.

PSALM III.

Lord, how are mine adversaries increased!
  Many are they that rise up against me.
Many there be which say of my soul,
There is no help for him in God.
  But thou, O Lord, art a shield about me;
  My glory, and the lifter up of my head.
I cry unto the Lord with my voice,
  And he answereth me out of his holy hill.

I laid me down and slept;
  I awaked; for the Lord sustaineth me.
I will not be afraid of ten thousands of the people,
That have set themselves against me round about.
  Arise, O Lord; save me, O my God;
For thou hast smitten all mine enemies upon the cheek bone;
  Thou hast broken the teeth of the wicked.
Salvation belongeth unto the Lord:
  Thy blessing be upon thy people.

PSALM IV.

Answer me when I call, O God of my righteousness;
Thou hast set me at large when I was in distress:
  Have mercy upon me, and hear my prayer.
O ye sons of men, how long shall my glory be turned into dishonour?
  How long will ye love vanity, and seek after falsehood?
But know that the Lord hath set apart him that is godly for himself:
  The Lord will hear when I call unto him.
Stand in awe, and sin not:
  Commune with your own heart upon your bed, and be still.
Offer the sacrifices of righteousness,
  And put your trust in the Lord.
Many there be that say, Who will show us any good?
  Lord, lift thou up the light of thy countenance upon us.
Thou hast put gladness in my heart,
  More than they have when their corn and their wine are increased.
In peace will I both lay me down and sleep:
  For thou, Lord, alone makest me dwell in safety.

PSALM V.

Give ear to my words, O Lord,
    Consider my meditation.
Hearken unto the voice of my cry, my King, and my God:
    For unto thee do I pray.
O Lord, in the morning shalt thou hear my voice;
    In the morning will I order my prayer unto thee, and will keep watch.
For thou art not a God that hath pleasure in wickedness:
    Evil shall not sojourn with thee.
    The arrogant shall not stand in thy sight:
Thou hatest all workers of iniquity.
Thou shalt destroy them that speak lies:
    The Lord abhorreth the bloodthirsty and deceitful man.
    But as for me, in the multitude of thy lovingkindness will I come into thy house:
In thy fear will I worship toward thy holy temple.
    Lead me, O Lord, in thy righteousness because of mine enemies;
Make thy way plain before my face.
    For there is no faithfulness in their mouth;
    Their inward part is very wickedness:
Their throat is an open sepulchre;
They flatter with their tongue.
    Hold them guilty, O God;
    Let them fall by their own counsels:
Thrust them out in the multitude of their transgressions;
For they have rebelled against thee.
    But let all those that put their trust in thee rejoice,
    Let them ever shout for joy, because thou defendest them;
Let them also that love thy name be joyful in thee.
    For thou wilt bless the righteous;
    O Lord, thou wilt compass him with favour as with a shield.

PSALM VI.

O Lord, rebuke me not in thine anger,
    Neither chasten me in thy hot displeasure.
Have mercy upon me, O Lord; for I am withered away:
    O Lord, heal me; for my bones are vexed.
My soul also is sore vexed:
And thou, O Lord, how long?
    Return, O Lord, deliver my soul:
    Save me for thy lovingkindness' sake.
For in death there is no remembrance of thee:
    In Sheol who shall give thee thanks?
I am weary with my groaning;
    Every night make I my bed to swim;
    I water my couch with my tears.
Mine eye wasteth away because of grief;
    It waxeth old because of all mine adversaries.
Depart from me, all ye workers of iniquity;
For the Lord hath heard the voice of my weeping.
    The Lord hath heard my supplication;
    The Lord will receive my prayer.
All mine enemies shall be ashamed and sore vexed:
    They shall turn back, they shall be ashamed suddenly.

PSALM VIII.

O Lord, our Lord,
How excellent is thy name in all the earth!
    Who hast set thy glory upon the heavens.
Out of the mouth of babes and sucklings hast thou established strength,
Because of thine adversaries,
    That thou mightest still the enemy and the avenger.
When I consider thy heavens, the work of thy fingers,

The moon and the stars, which thou hast ordained;
    What is man, that thou art mindful of him?
    And the son of man, that thou visitest him?
For thou hast made him but little lower than God,
    And crownest him with glory and honour.
Thou madest him to have dominion over the works of thy hands;
    Thou hast put all things under his feet:
All sheep and oxen,
Yea, and the beasts of the field;
    The fowl of the air, and the fish of the sea,
    Whatsoever passeth through the paths of the seas.
O Lord, our Lord,
How excellent is thy name in all the earth!

PSALM IX.

I will give thanks unto the Lord with my whole heart;
    I will show forth all thy marvellous works.
I will be glad and exult in thee:
    I will sing praise to thy name, O thou Most High.
When mine enemies turn back,
They stumble and perish at thy presence.
    For thou hast maintained my right and my cause;
Thou satest in the throne judging righteously.
    Thou hast rebuked the nations, thou hast destroyed the wicked,
Thou hast blotted out their name for ever and ever.
    The enemy are come to an end, they are desolate for ever;
And the cities which thou hast overthrown,
Their very memorial is perished.
    But the Lord sitteth as king for ever:
He hath prepared his throne for judgment.
    And he shall judge the world in righteousness,

He shall minister judgment to the peoples in uprightness.
>The Lord also will be a high tower for the oppressed,
A high tower in times of trouble;
>And they that know thy name will put their trust in thee:
For thou, Lord, hast not forsaken them that seek thee.
>Sing praises to the Lord, which dwelleth in Zion:
Declare among the people his doings.
>For he that maketh inquisition for blood remembereth them:
He forgetteth not the cry of the poor.
>Have mercy upon me, O Lord;
Behold my affliction which I suffer of them that hate me,
Thou that liftest me up from the gates of death;
>That I may show forth all thy praise:
In the gates of the daughter of Zion,
I will rejoice in thy salvation.
>The nations are sunk down in the pit that they made:
In the net which they hid is their own foot taken.
>The Lord hath made himself known, he hath executed judgment:
The wicked is snared in the work of his own hands.
>The wicked shall return to Sheol,
Even all the nations that forget God.
>For the needy shall not alway be forgotten,
Nor the expectation of the poor perish for ever.
>Arise, O Lord; let not man prevail:
Let the nations be judged in thy sight.
>Put them in fear, O Lord:
LET THE NATIONS KNOW THEMSELVES TO BE BUT MEN.

PSALM XI.

In the Lord put I my trust:
>How say ye to my soul,
Flee as a bird to your mountain?

For, lo, the wicked bend the bow,
They make ready their arrow upon the string,
   That they may shoot in darkness at the upright in heart.
If the foundations be destroyed,
What can the righteous do?
   The Lord is in his holy temple,
   The Lord, his throne is in heaven;
His eyes behold, his eyelids try, the children of men.
   The Lord trieth the righteous:
But the wicked and him that loveth violence his soul hateth.
   Upon the wicked he shall rain snares;
Fire and brimstone and burning wind shall be the portion of their cup.
   For the Lord is righteous; he loveth righteousness:
   The upright shall behold his face.

PSALM XII.

Help, Lord; for the godly man ceaseth;
   For the faithful fail from among the children of men.
They speak vanity every one with his neighbour:
   With flattering lip, and with a double heart, do they speak.
The Lord shall cut off all flattering lips,
   The tongue that speaketh great things:
Who have said, With our tongue will we prevail;
   Our lips are our own: who is lord over us?
For the spoiling of the poor, for the sighing of the needy,
Now will I arise, saith the Lord;
   I will set him in safety at whom they puff.
The words of the Lord are pure words;
   As silver tried in a furnace on the earth,
   Purified seven times.

Thou shalt keep them, O Lord,
Thou shalt preserve them from this generation for ever.
 The wicked walk on every side,
 When vileness is exalted among the sons of men.

PSALM XIII.

How long, O Lord, wilt thou forget me for ever?
 How long wilt thou hide thy face from me?
How long shall I take counsel in my soul,
Having sorrow in my heart all the day?
 How long shall mine enemy be exalted over me?
Consider and answer me, O Lord my God:
 Lighten mine eyes, lest I sleep the sleep of death;
Lest mine enemy say, I have prevailed against him;
 Lest mine adversaries rejoice when I am moved.
But I have trusted in thy mercy;
 My heart shall rejoice in thy salvation:
I will sing unto the Lord,
 Because he hath dealt bountifully with me.

PSALM XIV.

The fool hath said in his heart, There is no God.
 They are corrupt, they have done abominable works;
 There is none that doeth good.
The Lord looked down from heaven upon the children of men,
To see if there were any that did understand,
 That did seek after God.
They are all gone aside; they are together become filthy;
 There is none that doeth good, no, not one.

Have all the workers of iniquity no knowledge?
   Who eat up my people as they eat bread,
   And call not upon the Lord.
There were they in great fear:
   For God is in the generation of the righteous.
Ye put to shame the counsel of the poor,
   Because the Lord is his refuge.
Oh that the salvation of Israel were come out of Zion!
   When the Lord bringeth back the captivity of his people,
   Then shall Jacob rejoice, and Israel shall be glad.

PSALM XV.

Lord, who shall sojourn in thy tabernacle?
   Who shall dwell in thy holy hill?
He that walketh uprightly, and worketh righteousness,
   And speaketh truth in his heart.
He that slandereth not with his tongue,
Nor doeth evil to his friend,
   Nor taketh up a reproach against his neighbour.
In whose eyes a reprobate is despised;
   But he honoureth them that fear the Lord.
He that sweareth to his own hurt, and changeth not.
   He that putteth not out his money to usury,
   Nor taketh reward against the innocent.
HE THAT DOETH THESE THINGS SHALL NEVER BE MOVED.

PSALM XVI.

Preserve me, O God: for in thee do I put my trust.
   I have said unto the Lord, Thou art my Lord:
   I have no good beyond thee.

As for the saints that are in the earth,
They are the excellent in whom is all my delight.
  Their sorrows shall be multiplied that exchange the Lord for
    another god:
Their drink offerings of blood will I not offer,
  Nor take their names upon my lips.
The Lord is the portion of mine inheritance and of my cup:
Thou maintainest my lot.
  The lines are fallen unto me in pleasant places;
  Yea, I have a goodly heritage.
I will bless the Lord, who hath given me counsel:
  Yea, my reins instruct me in the night seasons.
I have set the Lord always before me:
  Because he is at my right hand, I shall not be moved.
Therefore my heart is glad, and my glory rejoiceth:
My flesh also shall dwell in safety.
  For thou wilt not leave my soul to Sheol;
  Neither wilt thou suffer thine holy one to see corruption.
Thou wilt show me the path of life:
  In thy presence is fulness of joy;
  In thy right hand there are pleasures for evermore.

PSALM XVIII.

I love thee, O Lord, my strength.
  The Lord is my rock, and my fortress, and my deliverer;
My God, my strong rock, in him will I trust;
  My shield, and the horn of my salvation, my high tower.
I will call upon the Lord, who is worthy to be praised:
  So shall I be saved from mine enemies.
The cords of death compassed me.
  And the floods of ungodliness made me afraid.

The cords of Sheol were round about me:
   The snares of death came upon me.
In my distress I called upon the Lord,
   And cried unto my God:
He heard my voice out of his temple,
   And my cry before him came into his ears.
Then the earth shook and trembled,
   The foundations also of the mountains moved and were shaken, because he was wroth.
There went up a smoke out of his nostrils, and fire out of his mouth devoured:
   Coals were kindled by it.
He bowed the heavens also, and came down;
   And thick darkness was under his feet.
And he rode upon a cherub, and did fly
   Yea, he flew swiftly upon the wings of the wind.
He made darkness his hiding place, his pavilion round about him;
   Darkness of waters, thick clouds of the skies.
At the brightness before him his thick clouds passed, hailstones and coals of fire.
   The Lord also thundered in the heavens,
And the Most High uttered his voice; hailstones and coals of fire.
   And he sent out his arrows, and scattered them;
Yea, lightnings manifold, and discomfited them.
   Then the channels of waters appeared, and the foundations of the world were laid bare, at thy rebuke, O Lord,
At the blast of the breath of thy nostrils.
   He sent from on high, he took me; he drew me out of many waters.
He delivered me from my strong enemy,
   And from them that hated me, for they were too mighty for me.

They came upon me in the day of my calamity:
  But the Lord was my stay.
He brought me forth also into a large place;
  He delivered me, because he delighted in me.
The Lord rewarded me according to my righteousness:
  According to the cleanness of my hands hath he recompensed me.
For I have kept the ways of the Lord,
  And have not wickedly departed from my God.
For all his judgments were before me,
  And I put not away his statutes from me.
I was also perfect with him,
  And I kept myself from mine iniquity.
Therefore hath the Lord recompensed me according to my righteousness,
  According to the cleanness of my hands in his eyesight.
With the merciful thou wilt show thyself merciful;
  With the perfect man thou wilt show thyself perfect;
With the pure thou wilt show thyself pure;
  And with the perverse thou wilt show thyself froward.
For thou wilt save the afflicted people;
  But the haughty eyes thou wilt bring down.
For thou wilt light my lamp:
  The Lord my God will lighten my darkness.
For by thee I run upon a troop;
  And by my God do I leap over a wall.
As for God, his way is perfect:
  The word of the Lord is tried; he is a shield unto all them that trust in him.
For who is God, save the Lord?
  And who is a rock beside our God?
The God that girdeth me with strength, and maketh my way perfect.
  He maketh my feet like hinds' feet: and setteth me upon my high places.

Thou hast also given me the shield of thy salvation:
>And thy right hand hath holden me up, and thy gentleness hath made me great.

Thou hast enlarged my steps under me, and my feet have not slipped.

PSALM XIX.

The heavens declare the glory of God;
>And the firmament showeth his handywork.

Day unto day uttereth speech,
>And night unto night showeth knowledge.

There is no speech nor language;
>Their voice cannot be heard.

Their line is gone out through all the earth,
>And their words to the end of the world.

In them hath he set a tabernacle for the sun,
>Which is as a bridegroom coming out of his chamber, and rejoiceth as a strong man to run his course.

His going forth is from the end of the heaven,
>And his circuit unto the ends of it: and there is nothing hid from the heat thereof.

The law of the Lord is perfect, restoring the soul:
>The testimony of the Lord is sure, making wise the simple.

The precepts of the Lord are right, rejoicing the heart:
>The commandment of the Lord is pure, enlightening the eyes.

The fear of the Lord is clean, enduring for ever:
>The judgments of the Lord are true, and righteous altogether.

More to be desired are they than gold, yea, than much fine gold:
>Sweeter also than honey and the honeycomb.

Moreover by them is thy servant warned:
>In keeping of them there is great reward.

Who can discern his errors?
>Clear thou me from hidden faults.

Keep back thy servant also from presumptuous sins;
  Let them not have dominion over me: then shall I be perfect, and I shall be clear from great transgression.
LET THE WORDS OF MY MOUTH AND THE MEDITATION OF MY HEART BE ACCEPTABLE IN THY SIGHT, O LORD, MY ROCK, AND MY REDEEMER.

PSALM XX.

The Lord answer thee in the day of trouble; the name of the God of Jacob set thee up on high;
  Send thee help from the sanctuary, and strengthen thee out of Zion;
We will triumph in thy salvation, and in the name of our God we will set up our banners:
  The Lord fulfil all thy petitions.
Now know I that the Lord saveth his anointed;
  He will answer him from his holy heaven with the saving strength of his right hand.
Some trust in chariots, and some in horses:
  But we will make mention of the name of the Lord our God.
They are bowed down and fallen: but we are risen, and stand upright.
  Save, Lord: let the King answer us when we call.

SELECTION FROM PSALM XXII.

I will declare thy name unto my brethren:
  In the midst of the congregation will I praise thee.
Ye that fear the Lord, praise him;
  All ye the seed of Jacob, glorify him; and stand in awe of him, all ye the seed of Israel.

For he hath not despised nor abhorred the affliction of the afflicted;
> Neither hath he hid his face from him; but when he cried unto him, he heard.

Of thee cometh my praise in the great congregation:
> I will pay my vows before them that fear him.

The meek shall eat and be satisfied: they shall praise the Lord that seek after him:
> Let your heart live for ever.

All the ends of the earth shall remember and turn unto the Lord:
> And all the kindreds of the nations shall worship before thee.

For the kingdom is the Lord's:
> And he is the ruler over the nations.

All the fat ones of the earth shall eat and worship:
> All they that go down to the dust shall bow before him, even he that cannot keep his soul alive.

A seed shall serve him;
> It shall be told of the Lord unto the next generation. They shall come and shall declare his righteousness unto a people that shall be born, that he hath done it.

PSALM XXIII.

The Lord is my shepherd; I shall not want.
> He maketh me to lie down in green pastures: he leadeth me beside the still waters.

He restoreth my soul:
> He guideth me in the paths of righteousness for his name's sake.

Yea, though I walk through the valley of the shadow of death, I will fear no evil; for thou art with me:
> Thy rod and thy staff, they comfort me.

Thou preparest a table before me in the presence of mine
    enemies:
    Thou hast anointed my head with oil; my cup runneth over.
Surely goodness and mercy shall follow me all the days of
    my life:
    And I will dwell in the house of the Lord for ever.

PSALM XXIV.

The earth is the Lord's, and the fulness thereof;
    The world, and they that dwell therein.
For he hath founded it upon the seas,
    And established it upon the floods.
Who shall ascend into the hill of the Lord?
    And who shall stand in his holy place?
He that hath clean hands, and a pure heart;
    Who hath not lifted up his soul unto vanity.
    And hath not sworn deceitfully.
He shall receive a blessing from the Lord,
    And righteousness from the God of his salvation.
This is the generation of them that seek after him,
    That seek thy face, O God of Jacob.
Lift up your heads, O ye gates;
    And be ye lift up, ye everlasting doors:
    And the King of glory shall come in.
Who is the King of glory?
    The Lord strong and mighty,
    The Lord mighty in battle.
Lift up your heads, O ye gates;
    Yea, lift them up, ye everlasting doors:
    And the King of glory shall come in.
Who is this King of glory?
    The Lord of hosts,
    He is the King of glory.

PSALM XXV.

Unto thee, O Lord, do I lift up my soul.
> O my God, in thee have I trusted,

Let me be not ashamed;
Let not mine enemies triumph over me.
> Yea, none that wait on thee shall be ashamed:
> They shall be ashamed that deal treacherously without cause.

Shew me thy ways, O Lord;
> Teach me thy paths.

Guide me in thy truth, and teach me;
> For thou art the God of my salvation;
> On thee do I wait all the day.

Remember, O Lord, thy tender mercies and thy lovingkindnesses:
> For they have been ever of old.

Remember not the sins of my youth, nor my transgressions:
> According to thy lovingkindness remember thou me,
> For thy goodness' sake, O Lord.

Good and upright is the Lord:
Therefore will he instruct sinners in the way.
> The meek will he guide in judgement:
> And the meek will he teach his way.

All the paths of the Lord are lovingkindness and truth
Unto such as keep his covenant and his testimonies.
> For thy name's sake, O Lord,
> Pardon mine iniquity, for it is great.

What man is he that feareth the Lord?
> Him shall he instruct in the way that he shall choose.

His soul shall dwell at ease;
> And his seed shall inherit the land.

The secret of the Lord is with them that fear him;
> And he will shew them his covenant.

Mine eyes are ever toward the Lord;
> For he shall pluck my feet out of the net.

Turn thee unto me, and have mercy upon me;
 For I am desolate and afflicted.
The troubles of my heart are enlarged:
 O bring thou me out of my distresses.
Consider mine affliction and my travail,
 And forgive all my sins.
Consider mine enemies, for they are many;
 And they hate me with cruel hatred.
O keep my soul, and deliver me:
 Let me not be ashamed, for I put my trust in thee.
Let integrity and uprightness preserve me.
For I wait on thee.
 Redeem Israel, O God,
 Out of all his troubles.

PSALM XXVI.

Judge me, O Lord, for I have walked in mine integrity:
 I have trusted also in the Lord without wavering.
Examine me, O Lord, and prove me;
 Try my reins and my heart.
For thy lovingkindness is before mine eyes;
 And I have walked in thy truth.
I have not sat with vain persons;
 Neither will I go in with dissemblers.
I hate the congregation of evil-doers,
 And will not sit with the wicked.
I will wash mine hands in innocency;
 So will I compass thine altar, O Lord:
That I may make the voice of thanksgiving to be heard,
 And tell of all thy wondrous works.
Lord, I love the habitation of thy house,
 And the place where thy glory dwelleth.

Gather not my soul with sinners,
Nor my life with men of blood:
> In whose hands is mischief,
> And their right hand is full of bribes.

But as for me, I will walk in mine integrity:
> Redeem me, and be merciful unto me.

My foot standeth in an even place:
> In the congregations will I bless the Lord.

PSALM XXVII.

The Lord is my light and my salvation; whom shall I fear?
> **The Lord is the strength of my life; of whom shall I be afraid?**

When evil-doers came upon me to eat up my flesh,
Even mine adversaries and my foes, they stumbled and fell.
> **Though an host should encamp against me,**
> **My heart shall not fear:**

Though war should rise against me,
> **Even then will I be confident.**

One thing have I asked of the Lord, that will I seek after;
> **That I may dwell in the house of the Lord all the days of my life,**
> **To behold the beauty of the Lord, and to inquire in his temple.**

For in the day of trouble he shall keep me secretly in his pavilion:
> **In the covert of his tabernacle shall he hide me;**
> **He shall lift me up upon a rock.**

And now shall mine head be lifted up above mine enemies round about me;
> **And I will offer in his tabernacle sacrifices of joy;**
> **I will sing, yea, I will sing praises unto the Lord.**

Hear, O Lord, when I cry with my voice:
> **Have mercy also upon me, and answer me.**

When thou saidst, Seek ye my face; my heart said unto thee,
Thy face, Lord, will I seek.
>   Hide not thy face from me;
>   Put not thy servant away in anger:
Thou hast been my help;
>   Cast me not off, neither forsake me, O God of my salvation.
>   For my father and my mother have forsaken me,
>   But the Lord will take me up.
Teach me thy way, O Lord;
>   And lead me in a plain path,
>   Because of mine enemies.
Deliver me not over unto the will of mine adversaries:
>   For false witnesses are risen up against me, and such as breathe out cruelty.
I had fainted, unless I had believed to see the goodness of the Lord
>   In the land of the living.
Wait on the Lord:
>   Be strong, and let thine heart take courage;
>   Yea, wait thou on the Lord.

PSALM XXVIII.

Unto thee, O Lord, will I call;
My rock, be not thou deaf unto me:
>   Lest, if thou be silent unto me,
>   I become like them that go down into the pit.
Hear the voice of my supplications, when I cry unto thee,
When I lift up my hands toward thy holy oracle.
>   Blessed be the Lord,
>   Because he hath heard the voice of my supplications.
The Lord is my strength and my shield,
>   My heart hath trusted in him, and I am helped:

Therefore my heart greatly rejoiceth;
And with my song will I praise him.
    The Lord is their strength,
    And he is a strong hold of salvation to his anointed.
Save thy people, and bless thine inheritance:
    Feed them also, and bear them up forever.

PSALM XXIX.

Give unto the Lord, O ye sons of the mighty,
    Give unto the Lord glory and strength.
Give unto the Lord the glory due unto his name;
Worship the Lord in the beauty of holiness.
    The voice of the Lord is upon the waters:
The God of glory thundereth,
Even the Lord upon many waters.
    The voice of the Lord is powerful;
    The voice of the Lord is full of majesty.
The voice of the Lord breaketh the cedars;
Yea, the Lord breaketh in pieces the cedars of Lebanon.
    He maketh them also to skip like a calf;
    Lebanon and Sirion like a young wild-ox.
The voice of the Lord cleaveth the flames of fire.
The voice of the Lord shaketh the wilderness;
    The Lord shaketh the wilderness of Kadesh.
The voice of the Lord maketh the hinds to calve,
And strippeth the forests bare:
    And in his temple every thing saith, Glory.
The Lord sat *as king* at the Flood;
Yea, the Lord sitteth as king for ever.
    The Lord will give strength unto his people;
    The Lord will bless his people with peace.

PSALM XXX.

I will extol thee, O Lord; for thou hast raised me up,
And hast not made my foes to rejoice over me.
> O Lord my God,
> I cried unto thee, and thou hast healed me.

O Lord, thou hast brought up my soul from Sheol:
> Thou hast kept me alive, that I should not go down to the pit.

Sing praise unto the Lord, O ye saints of his,
> And give thanks to his holy name.

For his anger is but for a moment;
In his favor is life:
> Weeping may tarry for the night,
> But joy cometh in the morning.

As for me, I said in my prosperity,
I shall never be moved.
> Thou, Lord, of thy favour hadst made my mountain to stand strong:
> Thou didst hide thy face; I was troubled.

I cried to thee, O Lord;
> And unto the Lord I made supplication:

What profit is there in my blood, when I go down to the pit?
> Shall the dust praise thee? shall it declare thy truth?

Hear, O Lord, and have mercy upon me:
> Lord, be thou my helper.

Thou hast turned for me my mourning into dancing;
> Thou hast loosed my sackcloth, and girded me with gladness:

To the end that my glory may sing praise to thee, and not be silent.
> O Lord my God, I will give thanks unto thee for ever.

PSALM XXXI.

In thee, O Lord, do I put my trust; let me never be ashamed:
    Deliver me in thy righteousness.
Bow down thine ear unto me; deliver me speedily:
    Be thou to me a strong rock, an house of defence to save me.
For thou art my rock and my fortress;
    Therefore for thy name's sake lead me and guide me.
Pluck me out of the net that they have laid privily for me;
    For thou art my strong hold.
Into thine hand I commend my spirit:
    Thou hast redeemed me, O Lord, thou God of truth.
I hate them that regard lying vanities:
But I trust in the Lord.
    I will be glad and rejoice in thy mercy:
    For thou hast seen my affliction;
Thou hast known my soul in adversities.
And thou hast not shut me up into the hand of the enemy;
    Thou hast set my feet in a large place.
Have mercy upon me, O Lord, for I am in distress:
    Mine eye wasteth away with grief, yea, my soul and my body.
    For my life is spent with sorrow, and my years with sighing:
But I trusted in thee, O Lord:
    I said, Thou art my God.
    My times are in thy hand:
Make thy face to shine upon thy servant:
    Save me in thy lovingkindness.
    Let me be not ashamed, O Lord; for I have called upon thee:
Oh how great is thy goodness, which thou hast laid up for them that fear thee,
    Which thou hast wrought for them that put their trust in thee, before the sons of men!
In the covert of thy presence shalt thou hide them from the plottings of man:

Thou shalt keep them secretly in a pavilion from the strife of tongues.
Blessed be the Lord:
For he hath shewed me his marvellous lovingkindness in a strong city.
As for me, I said in my haste, I am cut off from before thine eyes:
Nevertheless thou heardest the voice of my supplications when I cried unto thee.
O love the Lord, all ye his saints:
The Lord preserveth the faithful,
And plentifully rewardeth the proud doer.
BE STRONG, AND LET YOUR HEART TAKE COURAGE,
ALL YE THAT HOPE IN THE LORD.

PSALM XXXII.

Blessed is he whose transgression is forgiven, whose sin is covered.
Blessed is the man unto whom the Lord imputeth not iniquity,
And in whose spirit there is no guile.
When I kept silence, my bones waxed old
Through my roaring all the day long.
For day and night thy hand was heavy upon me:
My moisture was changed as with the drought of summer.
I acknowledged my sin unto thee, and mine iniquity have I not hid:
I said, I will confess my transgressions unto the Lord;
And thou forgavest the iniquity of my sin.
For this let every one that is godly pray unto thee in a time when thou mayest be found:
Surely when the great waters overflow they shall not reach unto him.

Thou art my hiding place; thou wilt preserve me from trouble;
   Thou wilt compass me about with songs of deliverance.
I will instruct thee and teach thee in the way which thou shalt go:
   I will counsel thee with mine eye upon thee.
Be ye not as the horse, or as the mule, which have no understanding:
   Whose trappings must be bit and bridle to hold them in,
   Else they will not come near unto thee.
Many sorrows shall be to the wicked:
   But he that trusteth in the Lord, mercy shall compass him about.
Be glad in the Lord, and rejoice, ye righteous:
   And shout for joy, all ye that are upright in heart.

PSALM XXXIII.

Rejoice in the Lord, O ye righteous:
   Praise is comely for the upright.
Give thanks unto the Lord with harp:
   Sing praises unto him with the psaltery of ten strings.
Sing unto him a new song;
   Play skilfully with a loud noise.
For the word of the Lord is right;
   And all his work is done in faithfulness.
He loveth righteousness and judgement:
   The earth is full of the lovingkindness of the Lord.
By the word of the Lord were the heavens made;
   And all the host of them by the breath of his mouth.
He gathereth the waters of the sea together as an heap:
   He layeth up the deeps in storehouses.
Let all the earth fear the Lord:
   Let all the inhabitants of the world stand in awe of him.

For he spake, and it was done;
  He commanded, and it stood fast.
The Lord bringeth the counsel of the nations to nought:
  He maketh the thoughts of the peoples to be of none effect.
The counsel of the Lord standeth fast for ever,
  The thoughts of his heart to all generations.
Blessed is the nation whose God is the Lord;
  The people whom he hath chosen for his own inheritance.
The Lord looketh from heaven;
He beholdeth all the sons of men;
  From the place of his habitation he looketh forth
  Upon all the inhabitants of the earth;
He that fashioneth the hearts of them all,
That considereth all their works.
  There is no king saved by the multitude of an host.
A mighty man is not delivered by great strength.
  An horse is a vain thing for safety:
  Neither shall he deliver any by his great power.
Behold, the eye of the Lord is upon them that fear him.
Upon them that hope in his mercy;
  To deliver their soul from death,
  And to keep them alive in famine.
Our soul hath waited for the Lord:
  He is our help and our shield.
For our heart shall rejoice in him,
  Because we have trusted in his holy name.
Let thy mercy, O Lord, be upon us,
  According as we have hoped in thee.

PSALM XXXIV.

I will bless the Lord at all times:
 His praise shall continually be in my mouth.
My soul shall make her boast in the Lord:
 The meek shall hear thereof, and be glad.
O magnify the Lord with me,
 And let us exalt his name together.
I sought the Lord, and he answered me,
And delivered me from all my fears.
 They looked unto him, and were lightened:
 And their faces shall never be confounded.
This poor man cried, and the Lord heard him,
And saved him out of all his troubles.
 The angel of the Lord encampeth round about them that fear him,
 And delivereth them.
O taste and see that the Lord is good:
 Blessed is the man that trusteth in him.
O fear the Lord, ye his saints:
 For there is no want to them that fear him.
The young lions do lack, and suffer hunger:
 But they that seek the Lord shall not want any good thing.
Come, ye children, and hearken unto me:
I will teach you the fear of the Lord.
 What man is he that desireth life,
 And loveth many days, that he may see good?
Keep thy tongue from evil,
And thy lips from speaking guile.
 Depart from evil, and do good;
 Seek peace, and pursue it.
The eyes of the Lord are toward the righteous,
And his ears are open unto their cry.
 The face of the Lord is against them that do evil,
 To cut off the remembrance of them from the earth.

The righteous cried, and the Lord heard,
And delivered them out of all their troubles.
>The Lord is nigh unto them that are of a broken heart,
>And saveth such as be of a contrite spirit.

Many are the afflictions of the righteous:
But the Lord delivereth him out of them all.
>He keepeth all his bones:
>Not one of them is broken.

Evil shall slay the wicked:
And they that hate the righteous shall be condemned.
>The Lord redeemeth the soul of his servants:
>And none of them that trust in him shall be condemned.

PSALM XXXVI.

The transgression of the wicked saith within my heart,
There is no fear of God before his eyes.
>For he flattereth himself in his own eyes,
>That his iniquity shall not be found out and be hated.

The words of his mouth are iniquity and deceit:
>He hath left off to be wise and to do good.

He deviseth iniquity upon his bed;
He setteth himself in a way that is not good;
>He abhorreth not evil.

Thy lovingkindness, O Lord, is in the heavens;
>Thy faithfulness reacheth unto the skies.

Thy righteousness is like the mountains of God;
>Thy judgements are a great deep:

O Lord, thou preservest man and beast.
>How precious is thy lovingkindness, O God!
>And the children of men take refuge under the shadow of thy wings.

They shall be abundantly satisfied with the fatness of thy house;
And thou shalt make them drink of the river of thy pleasures.
   For with thee is the fountain of life:
   In thy light shall we see light.
O continue thy lovingkindness unto them that know thee;
   And thy righteousness to the upright in heart.
Let not the foot of pride come against me,
And let not the hand of the wicked drive me away.
   There are the workers of iniquity fallen:
   They are thrust down, and shall not be able to rise.

PSALM XXXVII.

Fret not thyself because of evil-doers,
Neither be thou envious against them that work unrighteousness.
   For they shall soon be cut down like the grass,
   And wither as the green herb.
Trust in the Lord, and do good;
   Dwell in the land, and follow after faithfulness.
Delight thyself also in the Lord;
And he shall give thee the desires of thine heart.
   Commit thy way unto the Lord;
   Trust also in him, and he shall bring it to pass.
And he shall make thy righteousness to go forth as the light,
   And thy judgement as the noonday.
Rest in the Lord, and wait patiently for him:
   Fret not thyself because of him who prospereth in his way,
   Because of the man who bringeth wicked devices to pass.
Cease from anger, and forsake wrath:
Fret not thyself, it tendeth only to evil-doing.

For evil-doers shall be cut off:
But those that wait upon the Lord, they shall inherit the land.
For yet a little while, and the wicked shall not be:
Yea, thou shalt diligently consider his place, and he shall not be.
But the meek shall inherit the land;
And shall delight themselves in the abundance of peace.
The wicked plotteth against the just,
And gnasheth upon him with his teeth.
The Lord shall laugh at him:
For he seeth that his day is coming.
The wicked have drawn out the sword, and have bent their bows;
To cast down the poor and needy,
To slay such as be upright in the way:
Their sword shall enter into their own heart,
And their bows shall be broken.
Better is a little that the righteous hath
Than the abundance of many wicked.
For the arms of the wicked shall be broken:
But the Lord upholdeth the righteous.
The Lord knoweth the days of the perfect:
And their inheritance shall be for ever.
They shall not be ashamed in the time of evil:
And in the days of famine they shall be satisfied.
But the wicked shall perish,
And the enemies of the Lord shall be as the excellency of the pastures:
They shall consume; in smoke shall they consume away.
The wicked borroweth, and payeth not again:
But the righteous dealeth graciously, and giveth.
For such as be blessed of him shall inherit the land;
And they that be cursed of him shall be cut off.
A man's goings are established of the Lord;
And he delighteth in his way.

Though he fall, he shall not be utterly cast down:
For the Lord upholdeth him with his hand.
I have been young, and now am old;
Yet have I not seen the righteous forsaken,
Nor his seed begging their bread.
All the long day he dealeth graciously, and lendeth;
And his seed is blessed.
Depart from evil, and do good;
And dwell for evermore.
For the Lord loveth judgement,
And forsaketh not his saints;
They are preserved for ever:
But the seed of the wicked shall be cut off.
The righteous shall inherit the land,
And dwell therein for ever.
The mouth of the righteous talketh of wisdom,
And his tongue speaketh judgement.
The law of his God is in his heart;
None of his steps shall slide.
The wicked watcheth the righteous,
And seeketh to slay him.
The Lord will not leave him in his hand,
Nor condemn him when he is judged.
Wait on the Lord, and keep his way,
And he shall exalt thee to inherit the land:
When the wicked are cut off, thou shalt see it.
I have seen the wicked in great power,
And spreading himself like a green tree in its native soil.
But one passed by, and lo, he was not:
Yea, I sought him, but he could not be found.
Mark the perfect man, and behold the upright:
For the latter end of that man is peace.
As for transgressors, they shall be destroyed together:
The latter end of the wicked shall be cut off.

But the salvation of the righteous is of the Lord:
   He is their strong hold in the time of trouble.
And the Lord helpeth them, and rescueth them:
   He rescueth them from the wicked, and saveth them,
   Because they have taken refuge in him.

PSALM XXXIX.

I said, I will take heed to my ways,
That I sin not with my tongue:
   I will keep my mouth with a bridle,
   While the wicked is before me.
I was dumb with silence, I held my peace, even from good;
And my sorrow was stirred.
   My heart was hot within me;
While I was musing the fire kindled
Then spake I with my tongue:
Lord, make me to know mine end,
And the measure of my days, what it is;
   Let me know how frail I am.
Behold, thou hast made my days as handbreadths;
   And mine age is as nothing before thee:
Surely every man at his best estate is altogether vanity.
   Surely every man walketh in a vain show:
Surely they are disquieted in vain:
   He heapeth up riches, and knoweth not who shall gather them
And now, Lord, what wait I for?
My hope is in thee.
   Deliver me from all my transgressions:
   Make me not the reproach of the foolish.
I was dumb, I opened not my mouth;
Because thou didst it.

Remove thy stroke away from me:
I am consumed by the blow of thine hand.
When thou with rebukes dost correct man for iniquity,
Thou makest his beauty to consume away like a moth:
Surely every man is vanity.
Hear my prayer, O Lord, and give ear unto my cry;
Hold not thy peace at my tears:
For I am a stranger with thee,
A sojourner, as all my fathers were.
O spare me, that I may recover strength,
Before I go hence, and be no more.

PSALM XL.

I waited patiently for the Lord;
And he inclined unto me and heard my cry.
He brought me up also out of an horrible pit, out of the miry clay;
And he set my feet upon a rock, and established my goings.
And he hath put a new song in my mouth, even praise unto our God:
Many shall see it, and fear,
And shall trust in the Lord.
Blessed is the man that maketh the Lord his trust,
And respecteth not the proud, nor such as turn aside to lies.
Many, O Lord my God, are the wonderful works which thou hast done,
And thy thoughts which are to us-ward:
They cannot be set in order unto thee;
If I would declare and speak of them,
They are more than can be numbered.
Sacrifice and offering thou hast no delight in;
Mine ears hast thou opened:

Burnt offering and sin offering hast thou not required.
Then said I, Lo, I am come;
In the roll of the book it is written of me:
I delight to do thy will, O my God;
> Yea, thy law is within my heart.
I have published righteousness in the great congregation;
> Lo, I will not refrain my lips,
> O Lord, thou knowest.
I have not hid thy righteousness within my heart;
I have declared thy faithfulness and thy salvation:
> I have not concealed thy lovingkindness and thy truth from the great congregation.
Withhold not thou thy tender mercies from me, O Lord:
> Let thy lovingkindness and thy truth continually preserve me.
For innumerable evils have compassed me about,
Mine iniquities have overtaken me, so that I am not able to look up;
> They are more than the hairs of mine head, and my heart hath failed me.
Be pleased, O Lord, to deliver me:
Make haste to help me, O Lord.
> Let them be ashamed and confounded together
> That seek after my soul to destroy it:
Let them be turned backward and brought to dishonor
That delight in my hurt.
> Let them be desolate by reason of their shame
> That say unto me, Aha, Aha.
Let all those that seek thee rejoice and be glad in thee:
> Let such as love thy salvation say continually,
> The Lord be magnified.
But I am poor and needy;
Yet the Lord thinketh upon me:
> Thou art my help and my deliverer;
> Make no tarrying, O my God.

PSALM XLI.

Blessed is he that considereth the poor:
> The Lord will deliver him in the day of evil.

The Lord will preserve him, and keep him alive, and he shall be blessed upon the earth;
> And deliver not thou him unto the will of his enemies.

The Lord will support him upon the couch of languishing:
> Thou makest all his bed in his sickness.

I said, O Lord, have mercy upon me:
Heal my soul; for I have sinned against thee.
> Mine enemies speak evil against me, saying,
> When shall he die, and his name perish?

And if he come to see me, he speaketh vanity;
His heart gathereth iniquity to itself:
> When he goeth abroad, he telleth it.

All that hate me whisper together against me:
Against me do they devise my hurt.
> An evil disease, say they, cleaveth fast unto him:
> And now that he lieth he shall rise up no more.

Yea, mine own familiar friend, in whom I trusted, which did eat of my bread,
Hath lifted up his heel against me.
> But thou, O Lord, have mercy upon me, and raise me up,
> That I may requite them.

PSALM XLII.

As the heart panteth after the water brooks,
So panteth my soul after thee, O God.
> My soul thirsteth for God, for the living God:
> When shall I come and appear before God?

My tears have been my meat day and night,
While they continually say unto me, Where is thy God?

RESPONSIVE READINGS.   37

These things I remember, and pour out my soul within me,
How I went with the throng, and led them to the house of God,
With the voice of joy and praise, a multitude keeping holy-day.
Why art thou cast down, O my soul?
And why art thou disquieted within me?
Hope thou in God: for I shall yet praise him
For the health of his countenance.
O my God, my soul is cast down within me:
Therefore do I remember thee from the land of Jordan,
And the Hermons, from the hill Mizar.
Deep calleth unto deep at the noise of thy waterspouts:
All thy waves and thy billows are gone over me.
Yet the Lord will command his lovingkindness in the day-time,
And in the night his song shall be with me,
Even a prayer unto the God of my life.
I will say unto God my rock, Why hast thou forgotten me?
Why go I mourning because of the oppression of the enemy?
As with a sword in my bones, mine adversaries reproach me;
While they continually say unto me, Where is thy God?
Why art thou cast down, O my soul?
And why art thou disquieted within me?
Hope thou in God: for I shall yet praise him,
Who is the health of my countenance, and my God.

PSALM XLIII.

Judge me, O God, and plead my cause against an ungodly nation:
O deliver me from the deceitful and unjust man.
For thou art the God of my strength; why hast thou cast me off?

Why go I mourning because of the oppression of the enemy?
O send out thy light and thy truth; let them lead me:
    Let them bring me unto thy holy hill,
    And to thy tabernacles.
Then will I go unto the altar of God,
Unto God my exceeding joy:
    And upon the harp will I praise thee, O God, my God.
Why art thou cast down, O my soul?
And why art thou disquieted within me?
    Hope thou in God: for I shall yet praise him,
    Who is the health of my countenance, and my God.

PSALM XLV.

My heart overfloweth with a goodly matter:
I speak the things which I have made touching the king:
    My tongue is the pen of a ready writer.
Thou art fairer than the children of men;
Grace is poured into thy lips:
    Therefore God hath blessed thee for ever.
Gird thy sword upon thy thigh, O mighty one,
Thy glory and thy majesty.
    And in thy majesty ride on prosperously,
    Because of truth and meekness and righteousness:
And thy right hand shall teach thee terrible things.
    Thine arrows are sharp;
    The peoples fall under thee;
    They are in the heart of the king's enemies.
Thy throne, O God, is for ever and ever:
    A sceptre of equity is the sceptre of thy kingdom.
Thou hast loved righteousness, and hated wickedness:
    Therefore God, thy God, hath anointed thee
    With the oil of gladness above thy fellows.

All thy garments smell of myrrh, and aloes, and cassia:
> Out of ivory palaces stringed instruments have made thee glad.

Kings' daughters are among thy honorable women:
> At thy right hand doth stand the queen in gold of Ophir.

Hearken, O daughter, and consider, and incline thine ear;
> Forget also thine own people, and thy father's house;

So shall the king desire thy beauty:
For he is thy Lord; and worship thou him.
> And the daughter of Tyre shall be there with a gift;
> Even the rich among the people shall intreat thy favour.

The king's daughter within the palace is all glorious:
Her clothing is inwrought with gold.
> She shall be led unto the king in broidered work:
> The virgins her companions that follow her
> Shall be brought unto thee.

With gladness and rejoicing shall they be led:
They shall enter into the king's palace.
> Instead of thy fathers shall be thy children,
> Whom thou shalt make princes in all the earth.

I will make thy name to be remembered in all generations:
> Therefore shall the peoples give thee thanks for ever and ever.

PSALM XLVI.

God is our refuge and strength,
> A very present help in trouble.

Therefore will we not fear, though the earth do change,
And though the mountains be moved in the heart of the seas;
> Though the waters thereof roar and be troubled,
> Though the mountains shake with the swelling thereof.

There is a river, the streams whereof make glad the city of God,

The holy place of the tabernacles of the Most High.
> God is in the midst of her; she shall not be moved:

God shall help her, and that right early.
> The nations raged, the kingdoms were moved:
> He uttered his voice, the earth melted.

The Lord of hosts is with us;
> The God of Jacob is our refuge.

Come, behold the works of the Lord,
What desolations he hath made in the earth.
> He maketh wars to cease unto the end of the earth;
> He breaketh the bow, and cutteth the spear in sunder;
> He burneth the chariots in the fire.

Be still, and know that I am God:
> I will be exalted among the nations, I will be exalted in the earth.

The Lord of hosts is with us;
> The God of Jacob is our refuge.

PSALM XLVII.

O clap your hands, all ye peoples;
> Shout unto God with the voice of triumph.

For the Lord Most High is terrible;
> He is a great King over all the earth.

He shall subdue the peoples under us,
> And the nations under our feet.

He shall choose our inheritance for us,
The excellency of Jacob whom he loved.
> God is gone up with a shout,
> The Lord with the sound of a trumpet.

Sing praises to God, sing praises:
> Sing praises unto our King, sing praises.

For God is the King of all the earth:
> Sing ye praises with understanding.

God reigneth over the nations:
> God sitteth upon his holy throne.

The princes of the peoples are gathered together
To be the people of the God of Abraham:
> For the shields of the earth belong unto God;
> He is greatly exalted.

PSALM XLVIII.

Great is the Lord, and highly to be praised,
In the city of our God, in his holy mountain.
> Beautiful in elevation, the joy of the whole earth,
> Is mount Zion, on the sides of the north,
> The city of the great King.

God hath made himself known in her palaces for a refuge.
> For, lo, the kings assembled themselves,
> They passed by together.

They saw it, then were they amazed;
They were dismayed, they hasted away.
> Trembling took hold of them there;
> Pain, as of a woman in travail.

With the east wind
Thou breakest the ships of Tarshish.
> As we have heard, so have we seen
> In the city of the Lord of hosts, in the city of our God:

God will establish it for ever.
> We have thought on thy lovingkindness, O God,
> In the midst of thy temple.

As is thy name, O God,
So is thy praise unto the ends of the earth:
> Thy right hand is full of righteousness.

Let mount Zion be glad,
> Let the daughters of Judah rejoice,
> Because of thy judgements.

Walk about Zion, and go round about her:
Tell the towers thereof.
> Mark ye well her bulwarks,
> Consider her palaces;

That ye may tell it to the generation following.
> For this God is our God for ever and ever:
> He will be our guide even unto death.

PSALM LI.

Have mercy upon me, O God, according to thy lovingkindness:
> According to the multitude of thy tender mercies blot out my transgressions.

Wash me thoroughly from mine iniquity,
> And cleanse me from my sin.

For I acknowledge my transgressions:
> And my sin is ever before me.

Against thee, thee only, have I sinned,
And done that which is evil in thy sight:
> That thou mayest be justified when thou speakest,
> And be clear when thou judgest.

Behold, I was shapen in iniquity;
And in sin did my mother conceive me.
> Behold, thou desirest truth in the inward parts:
> And in the hidden part thou shalt make me to know wisdom.

Purge me with hyssop, and I shall be clean:
> Wash me, and I shall be whiter than snow.

Make me to hear joy and gladness;
That the bones which thou hast broken may rejoice.
> Hide thy face from my sins,
> And blot out all mine iniquities.

Create in me a clean heart, O God;

And renew a right spirit within me.
Cast me not away from thy presence;
And take not thy holy spirit from me.
Restore unto me the joy of thy salvation:
And uphold me with a free spirit.
Then will I teach transgressors thy ways;
And sinners shall be converted unto thee.
> Deliver me from bloodguiltiness, O God, thou God of my salvation;
> And my tongue shall sing aloud of thy righteousness.

O Lord, open thou my lips;
And my mouth shall shew forth thy praise.
For thou delightest not in sacrifice; else would I give it:
Thou hast no pleasure in burnt offering.
The sacrifices of God are a broken spirit:
A broken and a contrite heart, O God, thou wilt not despise.
Do good in thy good pleasure unto Zion:
Build thou the walls of Jerusalem.
Then shalt thou delight in the sacrifices of righteousness, in burnt offering and whole burnt offering:
Then shall they offer bullocks upon thine altar.

A SELECTION FROM PSALMS LV., LVI., LVII.

Give ear to my prayer, O God;
And hide not thyself from my supplication.
> Attend unto me, and answer me:
> I am restless in my complaint, and moan;

Because of the voice of the enemy,
Because of the oppression of the wicked;
> For they cast iniquity upon me,
> And in anger they persecute me.

My heart is sore pained within me:
And the terrors of death are fallen upon me.
> Fearfulness and trembling are come upon me,
> And horror hath overwhelmed me.

And I said, Oh that I had wings like a dove!
Then would I fly away, and be at rest.
> Lo, then would I wander far off,
> I would lodge in the wilderness.

I would hasten me to a shelter
From the stormy wind and tempest.
> As for me, I will call upon God;
> And the Lord shall save me.

Evening, and morning, and at noonday, will I complain, and moan:
And he shall hear my voice.
> Cast thy burden upon the Lord, and he shall sustain thee:
> He shall never suffer the righteous to be moved.

Put thou my tears into thy bottle;
Are they not in thy book?
> In God have I put my trust, I will not be afraid;
> What can man do unto me?

Thy vows are upon me, O God:
> I will render thank offerings unto thee.

For thou hast delivered my soul from death:
Hast thou not delivered my feet from falling?
> That I may walk before God
> In the light of the living.

Be merciful unto me, O God, be merciful unto me;
> For my soul taketh refuge in thee:
> Yea, in the shadow of thy wings will I take refuge,
> Until these calamities be overpast.

I will cry unto God Most High;
Unto God that performeth all things for me.
> He shall send from heaven, and save me.

My heart is fixed, O God, my heart is fixed:
> I will sing, yea, I will sing praises.

Awake up, my glory; awake, psaltery and harp:
I myself will awake right early.
> I will give thanks unto thee, O Lord, among the peoples:

I will sing praises unto thee among the nations.
> For thy mercy is great unto the heavens,
> And thy truth unto the skies.

Be thou exalted, O God, above the heavens;
> Let thy glory be above all the earth.

A SELECTION FROM PSALMS LXI., LXII., LXIII.

Hear my cry, O God;
Attend unto my prayer.
> From the end of the earth will I call unto thee, when my heart is overwhelmed:

Lead me to the rock that is higher than I.
> For thou hast been a refuge for me,
> A strong tower from the enemy.

I will dwell in thy tabernacle for ever:
> I will take refuge in the covert of thy wings.

For thou, O God, hast heard my vows:
> Thou hast given me the heritage of those that fear thy name.

My soul waiteth only upon God:
From him cometh my salvation.
> He only is my rock and my salvation:
> He is my high tower; I shall not be greatly moved.

My soul, wait thou only upon God;
For my expectation is from him.
He only is my rock and my salvation:
> He is my high tower; I shall not be moved.

With God is my salvation and my glory:
  The rock of my strength, and my refuge, is in God.
Trust in him at all times, ye people;
Pour out your heart before him:
  God is a refuge for us.
Surely men of low degree are vanity, and men of high
    degree are a lie:
  In the balances they will go up;
  They are together lighter than vanity.
Trust not in oppression,
And become not vain in robbery:
  If riches increase, set not your heart thereon.
God hath spoken once,
Twice have I heard this;
That power belongeth unto God:
  Also unto thee, O Lord, belongeth mercy:
  For thou renderest to every man according to his work.
O God, thou art my God; early will I seek thee:
  My soul thirsteth for thee, my flesh longeth for thee,
  In a dry and weary land, where no water is.
So have I looked upon thee in the sanctuary,
To see thy power and thy glory.
  For thy lovingkindness is better than life;
  My lips shall praise thee.
So will I bless thee while I live:
  I will lift up my hands in thy name.
My soul shall be satisfied as with marrow and fatness;
And my mouth shall praise thee with joyful lips;
  When I remember thee upon my bed,
  And meditate on thee in the night watches.
For thou hast been my help,
And in the shadow of thy wings will I rejoice.
  My soul followeth hard after thee:
  Thy right hand upholdeth me.

A SELECTION FROM PSALMS LXV., LXVI.

Praise waiteth for thee, O God, in Zion:
>And unto thee shall the vow be performed.
>O thou that hearest prayer,
>Unto thee shall all flesh come.

Iniquities prevail against me:
As for our transgressions, thou shalt purge them away.
>Blessed is the man whom thou choosest, and causest to approach unto thee,
>That he may dwell in thy courts:

We shall be satisfied with the goodness of thy house,
The holy place of thy temple.
>By terrible things thou wilt answer us in righteousness,
>O God of our salvation;

Thou that art the confidence of all the ends of the earth,
And of them that are afar off upon the sea:
>Which by his strength setteth fast the mountains;
>Being girded about with might:

Which stilleth the roaring of the seas, the roaring of their waves,
And the tumult of the peoples.
>They also that dwell in the uttermost parts are afraid at thy tokens:

Thou makest the outgoings of the morning and evening to rejoice.
>Thou visitest the earth, and waterest it,
>Thou greatly enrichest it;
>The river of God is full of water:

Thou providest them corn, when thou hast so prepared the earth.
>Thou waterest her furrows abundantly;
>Thou settlest the ridges thereof:

Thou makest it soft with showers;
Thou blessest the springing thereof.

Thou crownest the year with thy goodness;
And thy paths drop fatness.
They drop upon the pastures of the wilderness:
And the hills are girded with joy.
The pastures are clothed with flocks;
The valleys also are covered over with corn;
They shout for joy, they also sing.
Make a joyful noise unto God, all the earth:
Sing forth the glory of his name:
Make his praise glorious.
Say unto God, How terrible are thy works!
Through the greatness of thy power shall thine enemies submit themselves unto thee.
All the earth shall worship thee,
And shall sing unto thee;
They shall sing to thy name.
Come, and see the works of God;
He is terrible in his doing toward the children of men.
He turned the sea into dry land:
They went through the river on foot:
There did we rejoice in him.
He ruleth by his might for ever;
His eyes observe the nations:
Let not the rebellious exalt themselves.
O bless our God, ye peoples,
And make the voice of his praise to be heard:
Which holdeth our soul in life,
And suffereth not our feet to be moved.
For thou, O God, hast proved us:
Thou hast tried us, as silver is tried.
Come, and hear, all ye that fear God,
And I will declare what he hath done for my soul.
I cried unto him with my mouth,
And he was extolled with my tongue.

If I regard iniquity in my heart,
The Lord will not hear:
>   But verily God hath heard;
>   He hath attended to the voice of my prayer.

Blessed be God,
Which hath not turned away my prayer, nor his mercy from me.

A SELECTION FROM PSALMS LXVII., LXVIII., LXIX.

>   God be merciful unto us, and bless us,
>   And cause his face to shine upon us;

That thy way may be known upon earth,
>   Thy saving health among all nations.

Let the peoples praise thee, O God;
>   Let all the peoples praise thee.

O let the nations be glad and sing for joy:
For thou shalt judge the peoples with equity,
>   And govern the nations upon earth.

Let the peoples praise thee, O God;
>   Let all the peoples praise thee.

The earth hath yielded her increase:
God, even our own God, shall bless us.
>   God shall bless us;
>   And all the ends of the earth shall fear him.

Sing unto God, sing praises to his name:
>   Cast up a high way for him that rideth through the deserts;

His name is JAH; and exult ye before him.
>   A father of the fatherless, and a judge of the widows,
>   Is God in his holy habitation.

God setteth the solitary in families:
>   He bringeth out the prisoners into prosperity:
>   But the rebellious dwell in a parched land.

O God, when thou wentest forth before thy people,
When thou didst march through the wilderness;
    The earth trembled,
    The heavens also dropped at the presence of God:
Even yon Sinai trembled at the presence of God, the God of Israel.
    Thou, O God, didst send a plentiful rain,
    Thou didst confirm thine inheritance, when it was weary.
Thy congregation dwelt therein:
    Thou, O God, didst prepare of thy goodness for the poor.
The Lord giveth the word:
    The women that publish the tidings are a great host.
The chariots of God are twenty thousand, even thousands upon thousands:
    The Lord is among them, as in Sinai, in the sanctuary.
Thou hast ascended on high, thou hast led thy captivity captive;
Thou hast received gifts among men,
    Yea, among the rebellious also, that the Lord God might dwell with them.
Blessed be the Lord, who daily beareth our burden,
Even the God who is our salvation.
    God is unto us a God of deliverances;
    And unto Jehovah the Lord belong the issues from death.
They have seen thy goings, O God,
Even the goings of my God, my King, into the sanctuary.
    The singers went before, the minstrels followed after,
    In the midst of the damsels playing with timbrels.
Bless ye God in the congregations,
Even the Lord, ye that are of the fountain of Israel.
    Sing unto God, ye kingdoms of the earth;
    O sing praises unto the Lord;
To him that rideth upon the heavens of heavens, which are of old;

Lo, he uttereth his voice, and that a mighty voice.
    Ascribe ye strength unto God:
His excellency is over Israel,
    And his strength is in the skies.
O God, thou art terrible out of thy holy places:
    The God of Israel, he giveth strength and power unto his people.
BLESSED BE GOD.
I will praise the name of God with a song,
And will magnify him with thanksgiving.
    And it shall please the Lord better than an ox,
Or a bullock that hath horns and hoofs.
    The meek have seen it, and are glad:
Ye that seek after God, let your heart live.
    For the Lord heareth the needy,
    And despiseth not his prisoners.
Let Heaven and earth praise him,
The seas, and every thing that moveth therein.
    For God will save Zion, and build the cities of Judah;
    And they shall abide there, and have it in possession.
The seed also of his servants shall inherit it;
    And they that love his name shall dwell therein.

PSALM LXX.

Make haste, O God, to deliver me;
Make haste to help me, O Lord.
    Let them be ashamed and confounded
    That seek after my soul:
Let them be turned backward and brought to dishonour
That delight in my hurt.
    Let them be turned back by reason of their shame
    That say, Aha, Aha.

Let all those that seek thee rejoice and be glad in thee;
    And let such as love thy salvation say continually,
    Let God be magnified.
But I am poor and needy;
Make haste unto me, O God:
    Thou art my help and my deliverer;
    O Lord, make no tarrying.

PSALM LXXI.

In thee, O Lord, do I put my trust:
    Let me never be ashamed.
Deliver me in thy righteousness, and rescue me:
    Bow down thine ear unto me, and save me.
Be thou to me a rock of habitation, where unto I may continually resort:
    Thou hast given commandment to save me;
For thou art my rock and my fortress.
    Rescue me, O my God, out of the hand of the wicked,
    Out of the hand of the unrighteous and cruel man.
For thou art my hope, O Lord God:
Thou art my trust from my youth.
    By thee have I been holden up from the womb:
    Thou art he that took me out of my mother's bowels:
    My praise shall be continually of thee.
I am as a wonder unto many;
But thou art my strong refuge.
    My mouth shall be filled with thy praise,
    And with thy honour all the day.
Cast me not off in the time of old age;
    Forsake me not when my strength faileth.
For mine enemies speak concerning me;
    And they that watch for my soul take counsel together,
    Saying, God hath forsaken him:

Pursue and take him; for there is none to deliver.
> O God, be not far from me:
> O my God, make haste to help me.

Let them be ashamed and consumed that are adversaries to my soul;
> Let them be covered with reproach and dishonour that seek my hurt.

But I will hope continually,
And will praise thee yet more and more.
> My mouth shall tell of thy righteousness,

And of thy salvation all the day;
For I know not the numbers thereof.
> I will come with the mighty acts of the Lord God:

I will make mention of thy righteousness, even of thine only.
> O God, thou hast taught me from my youth;

And hitherto have I declared thy wondrous works.
> Yea, even when I am old and grayheaded, O God, forsake me not;

Until I have declared thy strength unto the next generation,
Thy might to every one that is to come.
> Thy righteousness also, O God, is very high;

Thou who hast done great things,
O God, who is like unto thee?
> Thou, which hast shewed us many and sore troubles,
> Shalt quicken us again,

And shalt bring us up again from the depths of the earth.
> Increase thou my greatness,
> And turn again and comfort me.

I will also praise thee with the psaltery,
Even thy truth, O my God:
> Unto thee will I sing praises with the harp,
> O thou Holy One of Israel.

My lips shall greatly rejoice when I sing praises unto thee;

And my soul, which thou hast redeemed.
> My tongue also shall talk of thy righteousness all the day long:

For they are ashamed, for they are confounded, that seek my hurt.

PSALM LXXII.

Give the king thy judgements, O God,
> And thy righteousness unto the king's son.

He shall judge thy people with righteousness,
> And thy poor with judgement.

The mountains shall bring peace to the people,
And the hills, in righteousness.
> He shall judge the poor of the people,
> He shall save the children of the needy,

And shall break in pieces the oppressor.
> They shall fear thee while the sun endureth,
> And so long as the moon, throughout all generations.

He shall come down like rain upon the mown grass:
> As showers that water the earth.

In his days shall the righteous flourish;
> And abundance of peace, till the moon be no more.

He shall have dominion also from sea to sea,
> And from the River unto the ends of the earth.

They that dwell in the wilderness shall bow before him;
> And his enemies shall lick the dust.

The kings of Tarshish and of the isles shall bring presents:
> The kings of Sheba and Seba shall offer gifts.

Yea, all kings shall fall down before him:
> All nations shall serve him.

For he shall deliver the needy when he crieth;
> And the poor, that hath no helper.

He shall have pity on the poor and needy,
> And the souls of the needy he shall save.

He shall redeem their soul from oppression and violence;
And precious shall their blood be in his sight:
And they shall live; and to him shall be given of the gold of Sheba:
    And men shall pray for him continually;
    They shall bless him all the day long.
There shall be abundance of corn in the earth upon the top of the mountains;
    The fruit thereof shall shake like Lebanon:
And they of the city shall flourish like grass of the earth.
    His name shall endure for ever;
    His name shall be continued as long as the sun:
And men shall be blessed in him;
All nations shall call him happy.
Blessed be the Lord God, the God of Israel,
Who only doeth wondrous things:
    And blessed be his glorious name for ever;
    And let the whole earth be filled with his glory.
Amen, and Amen.

PSALM LXXIII.

Surely God is good to Israel,
Even to such as are pure in heart.
    But as for me, my feet were almost gone;
    My steps had well nigh slipped.
For I was envious at the arrogant,
When I saw the prosperity of the wicked.
    For there are no bands in their death:
    But their strength is firm.
They are not in trouble as other men;
Neither are they plagued like other men.
    Therefore pride is as a chain about their neck;
    Violence covereth them as a garment.

Their eyes stand out with fatness:
They have more than heart could wish.
> They scoff, and in wickedness utter oppression:
> They speak loftily.
They have set their mouth in the heavens,
And their tongue walketh through the earth.
> Therefore his people return hither:
> And waters of a full cup are wrung out by them.
And they say, How doth God know?
And is there knowledge in the Most High?
> Behold, these are the wicked;
> And, being alway at ease, they increase in riches.
Surely in vain have I cleansed my heart,
And washed my hands in innocency;
> For all the day long have I been plagued,
> And chastened every morning.
If I had said, I will speak thus;
Behold, I had dealt treacherously with the generation of thy children.
> When I thought how I might know this,
> It was too painful for me;
Until I went into the sanctuary of God,
And considered their latter end.
> Surely thou settest them in slippery places:
> Thou castest them down to destruction.
How are they become a desolation in a moment!
They are utterly consumed with terrors.
> As a dream when one awaketh;
> So, O Lord, when thou awakest, thou shalt despise their image.
For my heart was grieved,
And I was pricked in my reins:
> So brutish was I, and ignorant;
> I was as a beast before thee.

Nevertheless I am continually with thee:
Thou hast holden my right hand.
    Thou shalt guide me with thy counsel,
    And afterward receive me to glory.
Whom have I in heaven but thee?
And there is none upon earth that I desire beside thee.
    My flesh and my heart faileth:
    But God is the strength of my heart and my portion for ever.
For, lo, they that are far from thee shall perish:
Thou hast destroyed all them that go a whoring from thee.
    But it is good for me to draw near unto God:
I have made the Lord God my refuge,
That I may tell of all thy works.

PSALM LXXVII.

I will cry unto God with my voice;
    Even unto God with my voice, and he will give ear unto me.
In the day of my trouble I sought the Lord:
    My hand was stretched out in the night, and slacked not;
    My soul refused to be comforted.
I remember God, and am disquieted:
    I complain, and my spirit is overwhelmed.
Thou holdest mine eyes watching:
I am so troubled that I cannot speak.
    I have considered the days of old,
    The years of ancient times.
I call to remembrance my song in the night:
    I commune with mine own heart;
    And my spirit made diligent search.
Will the Lord cast off for ever?
And will he be favourable no more?
    Is his mercy clean gone for ever?
    Doth his promise fail for evermore?

Hath God forgotten to be gracious?
> Hath he in anger shut up his tender mercies?

And I said, This is my infirmity;
But I will remember the years of the right hand of the Most High.
> I will make mention of the deeds of the Lord;
> For I will remember thy wonders of old.

I will meditate also upon all thy work,
And muse on thy doings.
> Thy way, O God, is in the sanctuary:

Who is a great god like unto God?
> Thou art the God that doest wonders:

Thou hast made known thy strength among the peoples.
> Thou hast with thine arm redeemed thy people,
> The sons of Jacob and Joseph.

The waters saw thee, O God;
The waters saw thee, they were afraid:
The depths also trembled.
> The clouds poured out water;
> The skies sent out a sound:
> Thine arrows also went abroad.

The voice of thy thunder was in the whirlwind;
> The lightnings lightened the world:
> The earth trembled and shook.

Thy way was in the sea,
And thy paths in the great waters,
And thy footsteps were not known.
> Thou leddest thy people like a flock,
> By the hand of Moses and Aaron.

PSALM LXXX.

Give ear, O Shepherd of Israel,
Thou that leadest Joseph like a flock;
    Thou that sittest upon the cherubim, shine forth.
Before Ephraim and Benjamin and Manasseh, stir up thy might,
And come to save us.
    Turn us again, O God;
    And cause thy face to shine, and we shall be saved.
O Lord God of hosts,
How long wilt thou be angry against the prayer of thy people?
    Thou hast fed them with the bread of tears,
    And given them tears to drink in large measure.
Thou makest us a strife unto our neighbours:
And our enemies laugh among themselves.
    Turn us again, O God of hosts;
    And cause thy face to shine, and we shall be saved.
Thou broughtest a vine out of Egypt:
Thou didst drive out the nations, and plantedst it.
    Thou preparedst room before it,
    And it took deep root, and filled the land.
The mountains were covered with the shadow of it,
And the boughs thereof were like cedars of God.
    She sent out her branches unto the sea,
    And her shoots unto the River.
Why hast thou broken down her fences,
So that all they which pass by the way do pluck her?
    The boar out of the wood doth ravage it,
    And the wild beasts of the field feed on it.
Turn again, we beseech thee, O God of hosts:
    Look down from heaven, and behold, and visit this vine,
    And the stock which thy right hand hath planted,

And the branch that thou madest strong for thyself,
It is burned with fire, it is cut down:
    They perish at the rebuke of thy countenance.
Let thy hand be upon the man of thy right hand,
    Upon the son of man whom thou madest strong for thyself.
So shall we not go back from thee:
    Quicken thou us, and we will call upon thy name.
    Turn us again, O Lord God of hosts;
CAUSE THY FACE TO SHINE, AND WE SHALL BE SAVED.

PSALM LXXXI.

Sing aloud unto God our strength:
    Make a joyful noise unto the God of Jacob.
Take up the psalm, and bring hither the timbrel,
The pleasant harp with the psaltery.
    Blow up the trumpet in the new moon,
    At the full moon, on our solemn feast day.
For it is a statute for Israel,
    An ordinance of the God of Jacob.
He appointed it in Joseph for a testimony,
When he went out over the land of Egypt:
Where I heard a language that I knew not.
    I removed his shoulder from the burden:
    His hands were freed from the basket.
Thou calledst in trouble, and I delivered thee;
    I answered thee in the secret place of thunder;
    I proved thee at the waters of Meribah.
Hear, O my people, and I will testify unto thee:
O Israel, if thou wouldest hearken unto me!
    There shall no strange god be in thee;
    Neither shalt thou worship any strange god.

I am the Lord thy God,
Which brought thee up out of the land of Egypt:
Open thy mouth wide, and I will fill it.
> But my people hearkened not to my voice;
> And Israel would none of me.
So I let them go after the stubbornness of their heart,
That they might walk in their own counsels.
> Oh that my people would hearken unto me,
> That Israel would walk in my ways!
I should soon subdue their enemies,
And turn my hand against their adversaries.
> The haters of the Lord should submit themselves unto him:
But their time should endure for ever.
> He should feed them also with the finest of the wheat:
> And with honey out of the rock should I satisfy thee.

PSALM LXXXIV.

How amiable are thy tabernacles,
O Lord of Hosts!
> My soul longeth, yea, even fainteth for the courts of the Lord;
My heart and my flesh cry out unto the living God.
> Yea, the sparrow hath found her an house,
> And the swallow a nest for herself, where she may lay her young,
Even thine altars, O Lord of hosts,
My King, and my God.
> Blessed are they that dwell in thy house:
> They will be still praising thee.
Blessed is the man whose strength is in thee;
> In whose heart are the high ways to Zion.
Passing through the valley of Weeping they make it a place of springs;

Yea, the early rain covereth it with blessings.
They go from strength to strength,
Every one of them appeareth before God in Zion.
O Lord God of hosts, hear my prayer:
Give ear, O God of Jacob.
Behold, O God our shield,
And look upon the face of thine anointed.
For a day in thy courts is better than a thousand.
I had rather be a doorkeeper in the house of my God,
Than to dwell in the tents of wickedness.
For the Lord God is a sun and a shield:
The Lord will give grace and glory:
No good thing will he withold from them that walk uprightly.
O LORD OF HOSTS,
BLESSED IS THE MAN THAT TRUSTETH IN THEE.

PSALM LXXXV.

Lord, thou hast been favorable unto thy land:
Thou hast brought back the captivity of Jacob.
Thou hast forgiven the iniquity of thy people,
Thou hast covered all their sin.
Thou hast taken away all thy wrath:
Thou hast turned thyself from the fierceness of thine anger.
Turn us, O God of our salvation,
And cause thine indignation toward us to cease.
Wilt thou be angry with us for ever?
Wilt thou draw out thine anger to all generations?
Wilt thou not quicken us again:
That thy people may rejoice in thee?
Shew us thy mercy, O Lord,
And grant us thy salvation.

I will hear what God the Lord will speak:
> For he will speak peace unto his people, and to his saints:

But let them not turn again to folly.
> Surely his salvation is nigh them that fear him;
> That glory may dwell in our land.

Mercy and truth are met together;
> Righteousness and peace have kissed each other.

Truth springeth out of the earth;
> And righteousness hath looked down from heaven.

Yea, the Lord shall give that which is good;
> And our land shall yield her increase.

Righteousness shall go before him;
> And shall make his footsteps a way to walk in.

PSALM LXXXVI.

Bow down thine ear, O Lord, and answer me;
> For I am poor and needy.

Preserve my soul; for I am godly:
> O thou my God, save thy servant that trusteth in thee.

Be merciful unto me, O Lord;
> For unto thee do I cry all the day long.

Rejoice the soul of thy servant;
> For unto thee, O Lord, do I lift up my soul.

For thou, Lord, art good, and ready to forgive,
And plenteous in mercy unto all them that call upon thee.
> Give ear, O Lord, unto my prayer;
> And hearken unto the voice of my supplications.

In the day of my trouble I will call upon thee;
For thou wilt answer me.
> There is none like unto thee among the gods, O Lord;
> Neither are there any works like unto thy works.

All nations whom thou hast made shall come and worship before thee, O Lord;

And they shall glorify thy name.
For thou art great, and doest wondrous things:
Thou art God alone.
Teach me thy way, O Lord; I will walk in thy truth:
Unite my heart to fear thy name.
I will praise thee, O Lord my God, with my whole heart;
And I will glorify thy name for evermore.
For great is thy mercy toward me;
And thou hast delivered my soul from the lowest pit.
O God, the proud are risen up against me,
And the congregation of violent men have sought after my soul,
And have not set thee before them.
But thou, O Lord, art a God full of compassion and gracious,
Slow to anger, and plenteous in mercy and truth.
O turn unto me, and have mercy upon me;
Give thy strength unto thy servant,
And save the son of thine handmaid.
Shew me a token for good;
That they which hate me may see it, and be ashamed,
Because thou, Lord, hast holpen me, and comforted me.

PSALM LXXXIX.

I will sing of the mercies of the Lord for ever:
With my mouth will I make known thy faithfulness to all generations.
For I have said, Mercy shall be built up for ever;
Thy faithfulness shalt thou establish in the very heavens.
I have made a covenant with my chosen,
I have sworn unto David my servant;
Thy seed will I establish for ever,
And build up thy throne to all generations.

And the heavens shall praise thy wonders, O Lord;
  Thy faithfulness also in the assembly of the holy ones.
For who in the skies can be compared unto the Lord?
  Who among the sons of the mighty is like unto the Lord?
A God very terrible in the council of the holy ones,
  And to be feared above all them that are round about him?
O Lord God of hosts,
Who is a mighty one, like unto thee, O JAH?
  And thy faithfulness is round about thee.
Thou rulest the pride of the sea:
  When the waves thereof arise, thou stillest them.
Thou hast broken Rahab in pieces, as one that is slain;
  Thou hast scattered thine enemies with the arm of thy strength.
The heavens are thine, the earth also is thine:
  The world and the fulness thereof, thou hast founded them.
The north and the south, thou hast created them:
  Tabor and Hermon rejoice in thy name.
Thou hast a mighty arm:
  Strong is thy hand, and high is thy right hand.
Righteousness and judgement are the foundation of thy throne:
  Mercy and truth go before thy face.
Blessed is the people that know the joyful sound:
  They walk, O Lord, in the light of thy countenance.
In thy name do they rejoice all the day:
  And in thy righteousness are they exalted.
For thou art the glory of their strength:
  And in thy favour our horn shall be exalted.
For our shield belongeth unto the Lord;
  And our king to the Holy One of Israel.
Then thou spakest in vision to thy saints,
And saidst, I have laid help upon one that is mighty;
  I have exalted one chosen out of the people.

I have found David my servant;
>   With my holy oil have I anointed him:

With whom my hand shall be established;
>   Mine arm also shall strengthen him.

The enemy shall not exact upon him;
>   Nor the son of wickedness afflict him.

And I will beat down his adversaries before him,
>   And smite them that hate him.

But my faithfulness and my mercy shall be with him;
>   And in my name shall his horn be exalted.

I will set his hand also on the sea,
>   And his right hand on the rivers.

He shall cry unto me, Thou art my father,
My God, and the rock of my salvation.
>   I also will make him my firstborn,
>   The highest of the kings of the earth.

My mercy will I keep for him for evermore,
>   And my covenant shall stand fast with him.

His seed also will I make to endure for ever,
>   And his throne as the days of heaven.

If his children forsake my law,
And walk not in my judgements;
>   If they break my statutes,
>   And keep not my commandments;

Then will I visit their transgression with the rod,
>   And their iniquity with stripes.

But my mercy will I not utterly take from him,
>   Nor suffer my faithfulness to fail.

My covenant will I not break,
>   Nor alter the thing that is gone out of my lips.

Once have I sworn by my holiness;
>   I will not lie unto David;

His seed shall endure for ever,
>   And his throne as the sun before me.

It shall be established for ever as the moon,
    And as the faithful witness in the sky.
BLESSED BE THE LORD FOR EVERMORE.
AMEN, AND AMEN.

PSALM XC.

Lord, thou hast been our dwelling place
In all generations.
    Before the mountains were brought forth,
    Or ever thou hadst formed the earth and the world,
Even from everlasting to everlasting, thou art God.
    Thou turnest man to destruction;
    And sayest, Return, ye children of men.
For a thousand years in thy sight
Are but as yesterday when it is past,
And as a watch in the night.
    Thou carriest them away as with a flood; they are as a sleep:
In the morning they are like grass which groweth up.
    In the morning it flourisheth, and groweth up;
    In the evening it is cut down, and withereth.
For we are consumed in thine anger,
    And in thy wrath are we troubled.
Thou hast set our iniquities before thee,
    Our secret sins in the light of thy countenance.
For all our days are passed away in thy wrath:
    We bring our years to an end as a tale that is told.
The days of our years are threescore years and ten,
Or even by reason of strength fourscore years;
    Yet is their pride but labour and sorrow;
    For it is soon gone, and we fly away.
Who knoweth the power of thine anger,
    And thy wrath according to the fear that is due unto thee?

So teach us to number our days,
That we may get us an heart of wisdom.
    Return, O Lord: how long?
    And let it repent thee concerning thy servants.
O satisfy us in the morning with thy mercy;
    That we may rejoice and be glad all our days.
Make us glad according to the days wherein thou hast afflicted us,
    And the years wherein we have seen evil.
Let thy work appear unto thy servants,
    And thy glory upon their children.
And let the beauty of the Lord our God be upon us:
    And establish thou the work of our hands upon us;
    Yea, the work of our hands establish thou it.

PSALM XCI.

He that dwelleth in the secret place of the Most High
Shall abide under the shadow of the Almighty.
    I will say of the Lord, He is my refuge and my fortress;
    My God, in whom I trust.
For he shall deliver thee from the snare of the fowler,
And from the noisome pestilence.
    He shall cover thee with his pinions,
    And under his wings shalt thou take refuge:
His truth is a shield and a buckler.
    Thou shalt not be afraid for the terror by night,
    Nor for the arrow that flieth by day;
For the pestilence that walketh in darkness,
Nor for the destruction that wasteth at noonday.
    A thousand shall fall at thy side,
    And ten thousand at thy right hand;

But it shall not come nigh thee.
Only with thine eyes shalt thou behold,
> And see the reward of the wicked.

For thou, O Lord, art my refuge !
> Thou hast made the Most High thy habitation;
> There shall no evil befall thee,

Neither shall any plague come nigh thy tent.
> For he shall give his angels charge over thee,
> To keep thee in all thy ways.

They shall bear thee up in their hands,
Lest thou dash thy foot against a stone.
> Thou shalt tread upon the lion and adder:

The young lion and the serpent shalt thou trample under feet.
> Because he hath set his love upon me, therefore will I deliver him:

I will set him on high, because he hath known my name.
> He shall call upon me, and I will answer him;

I will be with him in trouble:
> I will deliver him, and honour him.

With long life will I satisfy him,
> And shew him my salvation.

PSALM XCII.

It is a good thing to give thanks unto the Lord,
> And to sing praises unto thy name, O Most High:

To shew forth thy lovingkindness in the morning,
> And thy faithfulness every night,

With an instrument of ten strings, and with the psaltery;
> With a solemn sound upon the harp.

For thou, Lord, hast made me glad through thy work:
> I will triumph in the works of thy hands.

How great are thy works, O Lord!
Thy thoughts are very deep.
    A brutish man knoweth not;
    Neither doth a fool understand this:
When the wicked spring as the grass,
And when all the workers of iniquity do flourish;
    It is that they shall be destroyed for ever:
    But thou, O Lord, art on high for evermore.
For, lo, thine enemies, O Lord,
For, lo, thine enemies shall perish;
    All the workers of iniquity shall be scattered.
But my horn hast thou exalted like the horn of the wild-ox:
    I am anointed with fresh oil.
Mine eye also hath seen my desire on mine enemies,
    Mine ears have heard my desire of the evil-doers that rise up against me.
The righteous shall flourish like the palm tree:
    He shall grow like a cedar in Lebanon.
They that are planted in the house of the Lord
    Shall flourish in the courts of our God.
They shall still bring forth fruit in old age;
    They shall be full of sap and green:
To shew that the Lord is upright;
    He is my rock, and there is no unrighteousness in him.

PSALM XCIII.

The Lord reigneth; he is apparelled with majesty;
    The Lord is apparelled, he hath girded himself with strength:
The world also is stablished, that it cannot be moved.
    Thy throne is established of old:
Thou art from everlasting.

The floods have lifted up, O Lord,
The floods have lifted up their voice;
The floods lift up their waves.
Above the voices of many waters,
The mighty breakers of the sea,
The Lord on high is mighty.
Thy testimonies are very sure:
Holiness becometh thine house,
O Lord, for evermore.

PSALM XCV.

O come, let us sing unto the Lord:
Let us make a joyful noise to the rock of our salvation.
Let us come before his presence with thanksgiving,
Let us make a joyful noise unto him with psalms.
For the Lord is a great God,
And a great King above all gods.
In his hand are the deep places of the earth;
The heights of the mountains are his also.
The sea is his, and he made it;
And his hands formed the dry land.
O come, let us worship and bow down;
Let us kneel before the Lord our maker:
For he is our God,
And we are the people of his pasture, and the sheep of his hand.
To-day, Oh that ye would hear his voice!
Harden not your heart, as at Meribah,
As in the day of Massah in the wilderness:
When your fathers tempted me,
Proved me, and saw my work.
Forty years long was I grieved with that generation,
And said, It is a people that do err in their heart,

And they have not known my ways:
    Wherefore I sware in my wrath,
    That they should not enter into my rest.

PSALM XCVI.

O sing unto the Lord a new song:
    Sing unto the Lord, all the earth.
Sing unto the Lord, bless his name;
    Shew forth his salvation from day to day.
Declare his glory among the nations,
    His marvellous works among all the peoples.
For great is the Lord, and highly to be praised:
    He is to be feared above all gods.
For all the gods of the peoples are idols:
    But the Lord made the heavens.
Honour and majesty are before him:
    Strength and beauty are in his sanctuary.
Give unto the Lord, ye kindreds of the peoples,
    Give unto the Lord glory and strength.
Give unto the Lord the glory due unto his name:
    Bring an offering, and come into his courts.
O worship the Lord in the beauty of holiness:
    Tremble before him, all the earth.
Say among the nations, The Lord reigneth:
    The world also is stablished that it cannot be moved:
He shall judge the peoples with equity.
    Let the heavens be glad, and let the earth rejoice;
Let the sea roar, and the fulness thereof;
    Let the field exult, and all that is therein;
Then shall all the trees of the wood sing for joy;
    Before the Lord, for he cometh;

For he cometh to judge the earth:
  He shall judge the world with righteousness,
  And the peoples with his truth.

PSALM XCVII.

The Lord reigneth; let the earth rejoice;
  Let the multitude of isles be glad.
Clouds and darkness are round about him:
  Righteousness and judgement are the foundation of his throne.
A fire goeth before him,
  And burneth up his adversaries round about.
  His lightnings lightened the world:
  The earth saw, and trembled.
The hills melted like wax at the presence of the Lord,
  At the presence of the Lord of the whole earth.
The heavens declare his righteousness,
  And all the peoples have seen his glory.
Ashamed be all they that serve graven images,
That boast themselves of idols:
  Worship him, all ye gods.
Zion heard and was glad,
And the daughters of Judah rejoiced;
  Because of thy judgements, O Lord.
For thou, Lord, art most high above all the earth:
  Thou art exalted far above all gods.
O ye that love the Lord, hate evil:
  He preserveth the souls of his saints;
  He delivereth them out of the hand of the wicked.
Light is sown for the righteous,
  And gladness for the upright in heart.
Be glad in the Lord, ye righteous;
  And give thanks to his holy name.

PSALM XCVIII.

O sing unto the Lord a new song;
For he hath done marvellous things:
>His right hand, and his holy arm, hath wrought salvation for him.

The Lord hath made known his salvation:
>His righteousness hath he openly shewed in the sight of the nations.

He hath remembered his mercy and his faithfulness toward the house of Israel:
>All the ends of the earth have seen the salvation of our God.

Make a joyful noise unto the Lord, all the earth:
>Break forth and sing for joy, yea, sing praises.

Sing praises unto the Lord with the harp;
>With the harp and the voice of melody.

With trumpets and sound of cornet
Make a joyful noise before the King, the Lord.
>Let the sea roar, and the fulness thereof;

The world, and they that dwell therein;
>Let the floods clap their hands;

Let the hills sing for joy together;
Before the Lord, for he cometh to judge the earth:
>He shall judge the world with righteousness,
>And the peoples with equity.

PSALM XCIX.

The Lord reigneth; let the peoples tremble:
>He sitteth upon the cherubim; let the earth be moved.

The Lord is great in Zion;
>And he is high above all the peoples.

Let them praise thy great and terrible name:
Holy is he.
>The king's strength also loveth judgement;

Thou dost establish equity,
Thou executest judgement and righteousness in Jacob.
    Exalt ye the Lord our God,
    And worship at his footstool:
    Holy is he.
Moses and Aaron among his priests,
And Samuel among them that call upon his name;
They called upon the Lord, and he answered them.
    He spake unto them in the pillar of cloud:
They kept his testimonies, and the statute that he gave them.
    Thou answeredst them, O Lord our God:
Thou wast a God that forgavest them,
Though thou tookest vengeance of their doings.
    Exalt ye the Lord our God,
    And worship at his holy hill;
FOR THE LORD OUR GOD IS HOLY.

PSALM C.

Make a joyful noise unto the Lord, all ye lands.
    Serve the Lord with gladness:
Come before his presence with singing.
    Know ye that the Lord he is God:
It is he that hath made us, and we are his;
    We are his people, and the sheep of his pasture.
Enter into his gates with thanksgiving,
    And into his courts with praise:
Give thanks unto him, and bless his name.
    For the Lord is good; his mercy endureth for ever;
AND HIS FAITHFULNESS UNTO ALL GENERATIONS.

PSALM CII.

Hear my prayer, O Lord,
And let my cry come unto thee.
> Hide not thy face from me in the day of my distress:
Incline thine ear unto me;
In the day when I call answer me speedily.
> For my days consume away like smoke,
> And my bones are burned as a firebrand.
My heart is smitten like grass, and withered;
For I forget to eat my bread.
> By reason of the voice of my groaning
> My bones cleave to my flesh.
I am like a pelican of the wilderness;
> I am become as an owl of the waste places.
I watch, and am become
Like a sparrow that is alone upon the house top.
> Mine enemies reproach me all the day;
> They that are mad against me do curse by me.
For I have eaten ashes like bread,
And mingled my drink with weeping.
> Because of thine indignation and thy wrath:
For thou hast taken me up, and cast me away.
> My days are like a shadow that declineth;
> And I am withered like grass.
But thou, O Lord, shalt abide for ever;
> And thy memorial unto all generations.
Thou shalt arise, and have mercy upon Zion:
> For it is time to have pity upon her, yea, the set time is come.
For thy servants take pleasure in her stones,
> And have pity upon her dust.
So the nations shall fear the name of the Lord,
> And all the kings of the earth thy glory:

For the Lord hath built up Zion,
He hath appeared in his glory;
> He hath regarded the prayer of the destitute,
> And hath not despised their prayer.

This shall be written for the generation to come:
> And a people which shall be created shall praise the Lord.

For he hath looked down from the height of his sanctuary;
> From heaven did the Lord behold the earth;

To hear the sighing of the prisoner;
To loose those that are appointed to death;
> That men may declare the name of the Lord in Zion,
> And his praise in Jerusalem;

When the peoples are gathered together,
And the kingdoms, to serve the Lord.
> He weakened my strength in the way;
> He shortened my days.

I said, O my God, take me not away in the midst of my days:
> Thy years are throughout all generations.

Of old hast thou laid the foundation of the earth;
> And the heavens are the work of thy hands.

They shall perish, but thou shalt endure:
> Yea, all of them shall wax old like a garment;

As a vesture shalt thou change them, and they shall be changed:
> But thou art the same,
> And thy years shall have no end.

The children of thy servants shall continue,
> And their seed shall be established before thee.

PSALM CIII.

Bless the Lord, O my soul;
  And all that is within me, bless his holy name.
Bless the Lord, O my soul,
  And forget not all his benefits:
Who forgiveth all thine iniquities;
  Who healeth all thy diseases;
Who redeemeth thy life from destruction;
  Who crowneth thee with lovingkindness and tender mercies:
Who satisfieth thy mouth with good things;
  So that thy youth is renewed like the eagle.
The Lord executeth righteous acts,
  And judgements for all that are oppressed.
He made known his ways unto Moses,
  His doings unto the children of Israel.
The Lord is full of compassion and gracious,
Slow to anger, and plenteous in mercy.
  He will not always chide;
  Neither will he keep his anger for ever.
He hath not dealt with us after our sins,
  Nor rewarded us after our iniquities.
For as the heaven is high above the earth,
So great is his mercy toward them that fear him.
  As far as the east is from the west,
  So far hath he removed our transgressions from us.
Like as a father pitieth his children,
  So the Lord pitieth them that fear him.
For he knoweth our frame;
  He remembereth that we are dust.
As for man, his days are as grass;
As a flower of the field, so he flourisheth.
  For the wind passeth over it, and it is gone;
  And the place thereof shall know it no more.

But the mercy of the Lord is from everlasting to everlasting
    upon them that fear him,
  And his righteousness unto children's children;
To such as keep his covenant,
And to those that remember his precepts to do them.
  The Lord hath established his throne in the heavens;
  And his kingdom ruleth over all.
Bless the Lord, ye angels of his:
  Ye mighty in strength, that fulfil his word,
  Hearkening unto the voice of his word.
Bless the Lord, all ye his hosts;
  Ye ministers of his, that do his pleasure.
Bless the Lord, all ye his works,
In all places of his dominion:
  Bless the Lord, O my soul.

PSALM CIV.

Bless the Lord, O my soul.
  O Lord my God, thou art very great;
  Thou art clothed with honour and majesty.
Who coverest thyself with light as with a garment;
  Who stretchest out the heavens like a curtain:
Who layeth the beams of his chambers in the waters;
  Who maketh the clouds his chariot;
Who walketh upon the wings of the wind:
  Who maketh winds his messengers;
  His ministers a flaming fire:
Who laid the foundations of the earth,
That it should not be moved for ever.
  Thou coveredst it with the deep as with a vesture;
  The waters stood above the mountains.

At thy rebuke they fled;
　At the voice of thy thunder they hasted away;
They went up by the mountains, they went down by the valleys,
Unto the place which thou hadst founded for them.
　Thou hast set a bound that they may not pass over;
　That they turn not again to cover the earth.
He sendeth forth springs into the valleys;
They run among the mountains:
　They give drink to every beast of the field;
　The wild asses quench their thirst.
By them the fowl of the heaven have their habitation,
They sing among the branches.
　He watereth the mountains from his chambers:
　The earth is satisfied with the fruit of thy works.
He causeth the grass to grow for the cattle,
And herb for the service of man;
　That he may bring forth food out of the earth:
And wine that maketh glad the heart of man,
And oil to make his face to shine,
　And bread that strengtheneth man's heart.
The trees of the Lord are satisfied;
The cedars of Lebanon, which he hath planted;
　Where the birds make their nests:
　As for the stork, the fir trees are her house.
The high mountains are for the wild goats;
　The rocks are a refuge for the conies.
He appointed the moon for seasons:
　The sun knoweth his going down.
Thou makest darkness, and it is night;
Wherein all the beasts of the forest do creep forth.
　The young lions roar after their prey,
　And seek their meat from God.

The sun ariseth, they get them away,
And lay them down in their dens.
> Man goeth forth unto his work
> And to his labour until the evening.

O Lord, how manifold are thy works!
In wisdom hast thou made them all:
> The earth is full of thy riches.

Yonder is the sea, great and wide,
Wherein are things creeping innumerable,
Both small and great beasts.
> There go the ships;
> There is leviathan, whom thou hast formed to take his pastime therein.

These wait all upon thee,
That thou mayest give them their meat in due season.
> That thou givest unto them they gather;
> Thou openest thine hand, they are satisfied with good.

Thou hidest thy face, they are troubled;
> Thou takest away their breath, they die,
> And return to their dust.

Thou sendest forth thy spirit, they are created;
> And thou renewest the face of the ground.

Let the glory of the Lord endure for ever;
> Let the Lord rejoice in his works:

Who looketh on the earth, and it trembleth;
> He toucheth the mountains, and they smoke.

I will sing unto the Lord as long as I live:
> I will sing praise to my God while I have any being.

Let my meditation be sweet unto him:
> I will rejoice in the Lord.

Let sinners be consumed out of the earth.
And let the wicked be no more.
> Bless the Lord, O my soul.
> Praise ye the Lord.

PSALM CVII.

O give thanks unto the Lord; for he is good:
    For his mercy endureth for ever.
Let the redeemed of the Lord say so,
Whom he hath redeemed from the hand of the adversary;
    And gathered them out of the lands,
    From the east and from the west,
From the north and from the south.
    They wandered in the wilderness in a desert way;
    They found no city of habitation.
Hungry and thirsty,
Their soul fainted in them.
    Then they cried unto the Lord in their trouble,
    And he delivered them out of their distresses.
He led them also by a straight way,
That they might go to a city of habitation.
    Oh that men would praise the Lord for his goodness,
    And for his wonderful works to the children of men!
For he satisfieth the longing soul,
And the hungry soul he filleth with good.
    Such as sat in darkness and in the shadow of death,
    Being bound in affliction and iron;
Because they rebelled against the words of God,
And contemned the counsel of the Most High:
    Therefore he brought down their heart with labour;
    They fell down, and there was none to help.
Then they cried unto the Lord in their trouble,
And he saved them out of their distresses.
    He brought them out of darkness and the shadow of death,
    And brake their bands in sunder.
Oh that men would praise the Lord for his goodness,
And for his wonderful works to the children of men!
    For he hath broken the gates of brass,
    And cut the bars of iron in sunder.

Fools because of their transgression,
And because of their iniquities, are afflicted.
>Their soul abhorreth all manner of meat;
>And they draw near unto the gates of death.
Then they cry unto the Lord in their trouble,
And he saveth them out of their distresses.
>He sendeth his word, and healeth them,
>And delivereth them from their destructions.
Oh that men would praise the Lord for his goodness,
And for his wonderful works to the children of men!
>And let them offer the sacrifices of thanksgiving,
>And declare his works with singing.
They that go down to the sea in ships,
That do business in great waters;
>These see the works of the Lord,
>And his wonders in the deep.
For he commandeth, and raiseth the stormy wind,
Which lifteth up the waves thereof.
>They mount up to the heaven, they go down again to the depths:
>Their soul melteth away because of trouble.
They reel to and fro, and stagger like a drunken man,
And are at their wits' end.
>Then they cry unto the Lord in their trouble,
>And he bringeth them out of their distresses.
He maketh the storm a calm,
So that the waves thereof are still.
>Then are they glad because they be quiet;
>So he bringeth them unto the haven where they would be.
Oh that men would praise the Lord for his goodness,
And for his wonderful works to the children of men!
>Let them exalt him also in the assembly of the people,
>And praise him in the seat of the elders.
He turneth rivers into a wilderness,

And watersprings into a thirsty ground;
A fruitful land into a salt desert,
For the wickedness of them that dwell therein.
He turneth a wilderness into a pool of water,
And a dry land into watersprings.
And there he maketh the hungry to dwell,
That they may prepare a city of habitation;
And sow fields, and plant vineyards,
And get them fruits of increase.
He blesseth them also, so that they are multiplied greatly;
And he suffereth not their cattle to decrease.
Again, they are minished and bowed down
Through oppression, trouble, and sorrow.
He poureth contempt upon princes,
And causeth them to wander in the waste, where there is no way.
Yet setteth he the needy on high from affliction,
And maketh him families like a flock.
The upright shall see it, and be glad;
And all iniquity shall stop her mouth.
Whoso is wise shall give heed to these things,
And they shall consider the mercies of the Lord.

PSALM CX.

The Lord saith unto my lord, Sit thou at my right hand,
Until I make thine enemies thy footstool.
The Lord shall send forth the rod of thy strength out of Zion:
Rule thou in the midst of thine enemies.
Thy people offer themselves willingly in the day of thy power:
In the beauties of holiness, from the womb of the morning,
Thou hast the dew of thy youth.

The Lord hath sworn, and will not repent,
Thou art a priest for ever
After the order of Melchizedek.
> The Lord at thy right hand
> Shall strike through kings in the day of his wrath.

He shall judge among the nations,
He shall fill the places with dead bodies;
> He shall strike through the head in many countries.

He shall drink of the brook in the way:
> Therefore shall he lift up the head.

PSALM CXI.

Praise ye the Lord.
> I will give thanks unto the Lord with my whole heart,
> In the council of the upright, and in the congregation.

The works of the Lord are great,
Sought out of all them that have pleasure therein.
> His work is honour and majesty:

And his righteousness endureth for ever.
> He hath made his wonderful works to be remembered:

The Lord is gracious and full of compassion.
> He hath given meat unto them that fear him:
> He will ever be mindful of his covenant.

He hath shewed his people the power of his works,
In giving them the heritage of the nations.
> The works of his hands are truth and judgement;
> All his precepts are sure.

They are established for ever and ever,
They are done in truth and uprightness.
> He hath sent redemption unto his people;
> He hath commanded his covenant for ever:

Holy and reverend is his name.
The fear of the Lord is the beginning of wisdom;
A good understanding have all they that do thereafter:
His praise endureth for ever.

PSALM CXII.

Praise ye the Lord.
Blessed is the man that feareth the Lord,
That delighteth greatly in his commandments.
His seed shall be mighty upon earth.
The generation of the upright shall be blessed.
Wealth and riches are in his house:
And his righteousness endureth for ever.
Unto the upright there ariseth light in the darkness:
He is gracious, and full of compassion, and righteous.
Well is it with the man that dealeth graciously and lendeth;
He shall maintain his cause in judgement.
For he shall never be moved;
The righteous shall be had in everlasting remembrance.
He shall not be afraid of evil tidings:
His heart is fixed, trusting in the Lord.
His heart is established, he shall not be afraid,
Until he see his desire upon his adversaries.
He hath dispersed, he hath given to the needy;
His righteousness endureth for ever:
His horn shall be exalted with honour.
The wicked shall see it, and be grieved;
He shall gnash with his teeth, and melt away:
The desire of the wicked shall perish.

PSALM CXIII.

Praise ye the Lord.
Praise, O ye servants of the Lord,
Praise the name of the Lord.
>Blessed be the name of the Lord
>From this time forth and for evermore.

From the rising of the sun unto the going down of the same
The Lord's name is to be praised.
>The Lord is high above all nations,
>And his glory above the heavens.

Who is like unto the Lord our God,
That hath his seat on high,
>That humbleth himself to behold
>The things that are in heaven and in the earth?

He raiseth up the poor out of the dust,
>And lifteth up the needy from the dunghill;

That he may set him with princes,
Even with the princes of his people.
>He maketh the barren woman to keep house,
>And to be a joyful mother of children.

PRAISE YE THE LORD.

PSALM CXV.

Not unto us, O Lord, not unto us,
But unto thy name give glory,
>For thy mercy, and for thy truth's sake.

Wherefore should the nations say,
Where is now their God?
>But our God is in the heavens:
>He hath done whatsoever he pleased.

Their idols are silver and gold,
The work of men's hands.
> They have mouths, but they speak not;
> Eyes have they, but they see not;

They have ears, but they hear not;
Noses have they, but they smell not;
> They have hands, but they handle not;
> Feet have they, but they walk not;

Neither speak they through their throat.
They that make them shall be like unto them;
> Yea, every one that trusteth in them.

O Israel, trust thou in the Lord:
He is their help and their shield.
> O house of Aaron, trust ye in the Lord:
> He is their help and their shield.

Ye that fear the Lord, trust in the Lord:
He is their help and their shield.
> The Lord hath been mindful of us; he will bless us:

He will bless the house of Israel;
He will bless the house of Aaron.
> He will bless them that fear the Lord,
> Both small and great.

The Lord increase you more and more,
You and your children.
> Blessed are ye of the Lord,
> Which made heaven and earth.

The heavens are the heavens of the Lord;
> But the earth hath he given to the children of men.

The dead praise not the Lord,
Neither any that go down into silence;
> But we will bless the Lord
> From this time forth and for evermore.

PRAISE YE THE LORD.

PSALM CXVI.

I love the Lord, because he hath heard
My voice and my supplications.
    Because he hath inclined his ear unto me,
    Therefore will I call upon him as long as I live.
The cords of death compassed me,
And the pains of Sheol gat hold upon me:
    I found trouble and sorrow.
Then called I upon the name of the Lord;
O Lord, I beseech thee, deliver my soul.
    Gracious is the Lord, and righteous;
    Yea, our God is merciful.
The Lord preserveth the simple:
I was brought low, and he saved me.
    Return unto thy rest, O my soul;
    For the Lord hath dealt bountifully with thee.
For thou hast delivered my soul from death,
Mine eyes from tears,
And my feet from falling.
    I will walk before the Lord
    In the land of the living.
I believe, for I will speak:
I was greatly afflicted:
    I said in my haste,
    All men are a lie.
What shall I render unto the **Lord**
For all his benefits toward me?
    I will take the cup of salvation,
    And call upon the name of the Lord.
I will pay my vows unto the Lord,
Yea, in the presence of all his people.
    Precious in the sight of the Lord
    Is the death of his saints.

O Lord, truly I am thy servant:
I am thy servant, the son of thine handmaid;
Thou hast loosed my bonds.
> I will offer to thee the sacrifice of thanksgiving,
> And will call upon the name of the Lord.

I will pay my vows unto the Lord,
Yea, in the presence of all his people;
> In the courts of the Lord's house,
> In the midst of thee, O Jerusalem.

PRAISE YE THE LORD.

PSALM CXVII.

O praise the Lord, all ye nations;
Laud him, all ye peoples.
> For his mercy is great toward us;
> And the truth of the Lord endureth for ever.
> Praise ye the Lord.

PSALM CXVIII.

O give thanks unto the Lord; for he is good:
> For his mercy endureth for ever.

Let Israel now say,
> That his mercy endureth for ever.

Let the house of Aaron now say,
> That his mercy endureth for ever.

Let them now that fear the Lord say,
> That his mercy endureth for ever.

Out of my distress I called upon the Lord:
The Lord answered me and set me in a large place.

The Lord is on my side; I will not fear:
What can man do unto me?
It is better to trust in the Lord
Than to put confidence in man.
> It is better to trust in the Lord
> Than to put confidence in princes.

The Lord is my strength and song;
> And he is become my salvation,

The voice of rejoicing and salvation is in the tents of the righteous:
> The right hand of the Lord doeth valiantly.

The right hand of the Lord is exalted:
> The right hand of the Lord doeth valiantly.

I shall not die, but live,
And declare the works of the Lord.
> The Lord hath chastened me sore:
> But he hath not given me over unto death.

Open to me the gates of righteousness:
I will enter into them, I will give thanks unto the Lord.
> This is the gate of the Lord;
> The righteous shall enter into it.

I will give thanks unto thee, for thou hast answered me,
And art become my salvation.
> The stone which the builders rejected
> Is become the head of the corner.

This is the Lord's doing;
It is marvellous in our eyes.
> This is the day which the Lord hath made;
> We will rejoice and be glad in it.

Save now, we beseech thee, O Lord:
> O Lord, we beseech thee, send now prosperity.

Blessed be he that cometh in the name of the Lord:
> We have blessed you out of the house of the Lord.

PSALM CXIX.

Wherewithal shall a young man cleanse his way?
By taking heed thereto according to thy word.
With my whole heart have I sought thee:
O let me not wander from thy commandments.
Thy word have I laid up in mine heart,
That I might not sin against thee.
> Blessed art thou, O Lord:
> Teach me thy statutes.

With my lips have I declared
All the judgements of thy mouth.
> I have rejoiced in the way of thy testimonies,
> As much as in all riches.

I will meditate in thy precepts,
And have respect unto thy ways.
> I will delight myself in thy statutes:
> I will not forget thy word.

Deal bountifully with thy servant, that I may live;
So will I observe thy word.
> Open thou mine eyes, that I may behold
> Wondrous things out of thy law.

I am a sojourner in the earth:
Hide not thy commandments from me.
> My soul breaketh for the longing
> That it hath unto thy judgements at all times.

Thou hast rebuked the proud that are cursed,
Which do wander from thy commandments.
> Take away from me reproach and contempt;
> For I have kept thy testimonies.

Teach me, O Lord, the way of thy statutes;
And I shall keep it unto the end.
> Give me understanding, and I shall keep thy law;
> Yea, I shall observe it with my whole heart.

Make me to go in the path of thy commandments;
For therein do I delight.
> Incline my heart unto thy testimonies,
> And not to covetousness.

Turn away mine eyes from beholding vanity,
And quicken me in thy ways.
> Confirm thy word unto thy servant,
> Which belongeth unto the fear of thee.

Turn away my reproach whereof I am afraid;
For thy judgements are good.
> Behold, I have longed after thy precepts:
> Quicken me in thy righteousness.

Thou hast dealt well with thy servant,
O Lord, according unto thy word.
> Teach me good judgement and knowledge;
> For I have believed in thy commandments.

Before I was afflicted I went astray;
But now I observe thy word.
> Thou art good, and doest good;
> Teach me thy statutes.

It is good for me that I have been afflicted;
That I might learn thy statutes.
> The law of thy mouth is better unto me
> Than thousands of gold and silver.

Thy hands have made me and fashioned me:
Give me understanding, that I may learn thy commandments.
> They that fear thee shall see me and be glad;
> Because I have hoped in thy word.

I know, O Lord, that thy judgements are righteous,
And that in faithfulness thou hast afflicted me.
> Let, I pray thee, thy lovingkindness be for my comfort,
> According to thy word unto thy servant.

Let thy tender mercies come unto me, that I may live:
For thy law is my delight.
> Let the proud be ashamed; for they have overthrown me wrongfully:
> But I will meditate in thy precepts.

Let those that fear thee turn unto me,
And they shall know thy testimonies.
> Let my heart be perfect in thy statutes;
> That I be not ashamed.

For ever, O Lord,
Thy word is settled in heaven.
> Thy faithfulness is unto all generations:
> Thou hast established the earth, and it abideth.

They abide this day according to thine ordinances;
For all things are thy servants.
> Unless thy law had been my delight,
> I should then have perished in mine affliction.

I will never forget thy precepts;
For with them thou hast quickened me.
> I am thine, save me;
> For I have sought thy precepts.

The wicked have waited for me to destroy me;
But I will consider thy testimonies.
> I have seen an end of all perfection;
> But thy commandment is exceeding broad.

Oh how I love thy law!
It is my meditation all the day.
> Thy commandments make me wiser than mine enemies;
> For they are ever with me.

I have more understanding than all my teachers;
For thy testimonies are my meditation.
> I understand more than the aged,
> Because I have kept thy precepts.

I have refrained my feet from every evil way,

That I might observe thy word.
> I have not turned aside from thy judgements;
> For thou hast taught me.

How sweet are thy words unto my taste!
Yea, sweeter than honey to my mouth!
> Through thy precepts I get understanding:
> Therefore I hate every false way.

Thy word is a lamp unto my feet,
And light unto my path.
> I have sworn, and have confirmed it,
> That I will observe thy righteous judgements.

I am afflicted very much:
Quicken me, O Lord, according unto thy word.
> Accept, I beseech thee, the freewill offerings of my mouth, O Lord,
> And teach me thy judgements.

My soul is continually in my hand;
Yet do I not forget thy law.
> The wicked have laid a snare for me;
> Yet went I not astray from thy precepts.

Thy testimonies have I taken as an heritage for ever;
For they are the rejoicing of my heart.
> I have inclined mind heart to perform thy statutes,
> For ever, even unto the end.

PSALM CXXI.

I will lift up mine eyes unto the mountains:
From whence shall my help come?
> My help cometh from the Lord,
> Which made heaven and earth.

He will not suffer thy foot to be moved:
He that keepeth thee will not slumber.

>   Behold, he that keepeth Israel
>   Shall neither slumber nor sleep.
>
> The Lord is thy keeper:
> The Lord is thy shade upon thy right hand.
>
>   The sun shall not smite thee by day,
>   Nor the moon by night.
>
> The Lord shall keep thee from all evil;
> He shall keep thy soul.
>
>   The Lord shall keep thy going out and thy coming in,
>   From this time forth and for evermore.

PSALM CXXII.

> I was glad when they said unto me,
> Let us go unto the house of the Lord.
>
>   Our feet are standing
>   Within thy gates, O Jerusalem;
>
> Jerusalem, that art builded
> As a city that is compact together:
>
>   Whither the tribes go up, even the tribes of the Lord,
>   For a testimony unto Israel,
>   To give thanks unto the name of the Lord.
>
> For there are set thrones for judgement,
> The thrones of the house of David.
>
>   Pray for the peace of Jerusalem:
>
> They shall prosper that love thee.
>
>   Peace be within thy walls,
>   And prosperity within thy palaces.
>
> For my brethren and companions' sakes,
> I will now say, Peace be within thee.
>
>   For the sake of the house of the Lord our God
>   I will seek thy good.

PSALM CXXIV.

If it had not been the Lord who was on our side,
Let Israel now say:
    If it had not been the Lord who was on our side,
    When men rose up against us:
Then they had swallowed us up alive,
When their wrath was kindled against us:
    Then the waters had overwhelmed us,
    The stream had gone over our soul:
Then the proud waters had gone over our soul.
    Blessed be the Lord,
    Who hath not given us as a prey to their teeth.
Our soul is escaped as a bird out of the snare of the fowlers:
The snare is broken, and we are escaped.
    Our help is in the name of the Lord,
    Who made heaven and earth.

PSALM CXXV.

They that trust in the Lord
Are as mount Zion, which cannot be moved, but abideth for ever.
    As the mountains are round about Jerusalem,
    So the Lord is round about his people,
    From this time forth and for evermore.
For the sceptre of wickedness shall not rest upon the lot of the righteous;
That the righteous put not forth their hands unto iniquity.
    Do good, O Lord, unto those that be good,
    And to them that are upright in their hearts.
But as for such as turn aside unto their crooked ways,
The Lord shall lead them forth with the workers of iniquity.
    Peace be upon Israel.

PSALM CXXVI.

When the Lord turned again the captivity of Zion,
We were like unto them that dream.
    Then was our mouth filled with laughter,
    And our tongue with singing:
Then said they among the nations,
The Lord hath done great things for them.
    The Lord hath done great things for us;
    Whereof we are glad.
Turn again our captivity, O Lord,
As the streams in the South.
    They that sow in tears shall reap in joy.
Though he goeth on his way weeping, bearing forth the seed;
He shall come again with joy, bringing his sheaves with him.

PSALM CXXVII.

Except the Lord build the house,
They labour in vain that build it:
    Except the Lord keep the city,
    The watchman waketh but in vain.
It is vain for you that ye rise up early, and so late take rest,
And eat the bread of toil:
    For so he giveth unto his beloved sleep.
Lo, children are an heritage of the Lord:
And the fruit of the womb is his reward.
    As arrows in the hand of a mighty man,
    So are the children of youth.
Happy is the man that hath his quiver full of them:
They shall not be ashamed,
When they speak with their enemies in the gate.

PSALM CXXVIII.

Blessed is every one that feareth the Lord,
That walketh in his ways.
> For thou shalt eat the labour of thine hands:
> Happy shalt thou be, and it shall be well with thee.

Thy wife shall be as a fruitful vine, in the innermost parts of thine house:
Thy children like olive plants, round about thy table.
> Behold, that thus shall the man be blessed
> That feareth the Lord.

The Lord shall bless thee out of Zion:
And thou shalt see the good of Jerusalem all the days of thy life.
> Yea, thou shalt see thy children's children.
> Peace be upon Israel.

PSALM CXXX.

Out of the depths have I cried unto thee, O Lord.
> Lord, hear my voice:
> Let thine ears be attentive
> To the voice of my supplications.

If thou, Lord, shouldest mark iniquities,
O Lord, who shall stand?
> But there is forgiveness with thee,
> That thou mayest be feared.

I wait for the Lord, my soul doth wait,
And in his word do I hope.
> My soul looketh for the Lord,
> More than watchmen look for the morning;
> Yea, more than watchmen for the morning.

O Israel, hope in the Lord;

For with the Lord there is mercy,
And with him is plenteous redemption.
    And he shall redeem Israel
    From all his iniquities.

PSALM CXXXI.

Lord, my heart is not haughty, nor mine eyes lofty;
Neither do I exercise myself in great matters,
    Or in things too wonderful for me.
    Surely I have stilled and quieted my soul;
Like a weaned child with his mother,
My soul is with me like a weaned child.
    O Israel, hope in the Lord
    From this time forth and for evermore.

PSALM CXXXII.

Lord, remember for David
All his affliction;
    How he sware unto the Lord,
    And vowed unto the Mighty One of Jacob:
Surely I will not come into the tabernacle of my house,
Nor go up into my bed;
    I will not give sleep to mine eyes,
    Or slumber to mine eyelids;
Until I find out a place for the Lord,
A tabernacle for the Mighty One of Jacob.
    Lo, we heard of it in Ephrathah:
    We found it in the field of the wood.
We will go into his tabernacles;
We will worship at his footstool.

Arise, O Lord, into thy resting place;
Thou, and the ark of thy strength.
Let thy priests be clothed with righteousness;
And let thy saints shout for joy.
For thy servant David's sake
Turn not away the face of thine anointed.
The Lord hath sworn unto David in truth;
He will not turn from it:
Of the fruit of thy body will I set upon thy throne.
If thy children will keep my covenant
And my testimony that I shall teach them,
Their children also shall sit upon thy throne for evermore.
For the Lord hath chosen Zion;
He hath desired it for his habitation.
This is my resting place for ever:
Here will I dwell; for I have desired it.
I will abundantly bless her provision:
I will satisfy her poor with bread.
Her priests also will I clothe with salvation:
And her saints shall shout aloud for joy.
There will I make the horn of David to bud:
I have ordained a lamp for mine anointed.
His enemies will I clothe with shame:
But upon himself shall his crown flourish.

PSALM CXXXIII.

Behold, how good and how pleasant it is
For brethren to dwell together in unity!
It is like the precious oil upon the head,
That ran down upon the beard,
Even Aaron's beard;
That came down upon the skirt of his garments;

Like the dew of Hermon,
That cometh down upon the mountains of Zion:
> For there the Lord commanded the blessing,
> Even life for evermore.

PSALM CXXXIV.

Behold, bless ye the Lord, all ye servants of the Lord,
Which by night stand in the house of the Lord.
> Lift up your hands to the sanctuary,
> And bless ye the Lord.

The Lord bless thee out of Zion;
> Even he that made heaven and earth.

PSALM CXXXV.

Praise ye the Lord.
Praise ye the name of the Lord;
> Praise him, O ye servants of the Lord:
> Ye that stand in the house of the Lord,
> In the courts of the house of our God.

Praise ye the Lord; for the Lord is good:
> Sing praises unto his name; for it is pleasant.

For the Lord hath chosen Jacob unto himself,
And Israel for his peculiar treasure.
> For I know that the Lord is great,
> And that our Lord is above all gods.

Whatsoever the Lord pleased, that hath he done,
In heaven and in earth, in the seas and in all deeps.
> He causeth the vapours to ascend from the ends of the earth;
> He maketh lightnings for the rain;

He bringeth forth the wind out of his treasuries.
> Ye that fear the Lord, bless ye the Lord.

Blessed be the Lord out of Zion,
Who dwelleth at Jerusalem.
PRAISE YE THE LORD.

PSALM CXXXVIII.

I will give thee thanks with my whole heart:
Before the gods will I sing praises unto thee.
    I will worship toward thy holy temple,
    And give thanks unto thy name for thy lovingkindness and for thy truth:
For thou hast magnified thy word above all thy name.
    In the day that I called thou answeredst me,
    Thou didst encourage me with strength in my soul.
All the kings of the earth shall give thee thanks, O Lord,
For they have heard the words of thy mouth.
    Yea, they shall sing of the ways of the Lord;
    For great is the glory of the Lord.
For though the Lord be high, yet hath he respect unto the lowly:
    But the haughty he knoweth from afar.
Though I walk in the midst of trouble, thou wilt revive me;
    Thou shalt stretch forth thine hand against the wrath of mine enemies,
    And thy right hand shall save me.
The Lord will perfect that which concerneth me:
Thy mercy, O Lord, endureth for ever;
    Forsake not the works of thine own hands.

PSALM CXXXIX.

O Lord, thou hast searched me, and known me.
    Thou knowest my downsitting and mine uprising,
    Thou understandest my thought afar off.
Thou searchest out my path and my lying down,
And art acquainted with all my ways.
    For there is not a word in my tongue,
    But, lo, O Lord, thou knowest it altogether.
Thou hast beset me behind and before,
And laid thine hand upon me.
    Such knowledge is too wonderful for me;
    It is high, I cannot attain unto it.
Whither shall I go from thy spirit?
Or whither shall I flee from thy presence?
    If I ascend up into heaven, thou art there:
    If I make my bed in Sheol, behold, thou art there.
If I take the wings of the morning,
And dwell in the uttermost parts of the sea;
Even there shall thy hand lead me,
And thy right hand shall hold me.
    If I say, Surely the darkness shall overwhelm me,
    And the light about me shall be night;
Even the darkness hideth not from thee,
But the night shineth as the day:
    The darkness and the light are both alike to thee.
For thou hast possessed my reins:
Thou hast covered me in my mother's womb.
    I will give thanks unto thee; for I am fearfully and wonderfully made:
Wonderful are thy works;
And that my soul knoweth right well.
    My frame was not hidden from thee,
    When I was made in secret,
    And curiously wrought in the lowest parts of the earth.

Thine eyes did see mine unperfect substance,
And in thy book were all my members written,
Which day by day were fashioned,
When as yet there was none of them.
>How precious also are thy thoughts unto me, O God!
>How great is the sum of them!

If I should count them, they are more in number than the sand:
>When I awake, I am still with thee.

Surely thou wilt slay the wicked, O God:
Depart from me therefore, ye bloodthirsty men.
>For they speak against thee wickedly,
>And thine enemies take thy name in vain.

Do not I hate them, O Lord, that hate thee?
And am not I grieved with those that rise up against thee?
>I hate them with perfect hatred:
>I count them mine enemies.

Search me, O God, and know my heart:
Try me, and know my thoughts:
>And see if there be any way of wickedness in me,
>And lead me in the way everlasting.

PSALM CXL.

I said unto the Lord, Thou art my God:
>Give ear unto the voice of my supplications, O Lord.

I know that the Lord will maintain the cause of the afflicted,
And the right of the needy.
>Surely the righteous shall give thanks unto thy name:
>The upright shall dwell in thy presence.

PSALM CXLI.

Lord, I have called upon thee; make haste unto me:
    Give ear unto my voice, when I call unto thee.
Let my prayer be set forth as incense before thee;
    The lifting up of my hands as the evening sacrifice.
For mine eyes are unto thee, O God the Lord:
    In thee do I put my trust; leave not my soul destitute.

PSALM CXLII.

I cry with my voice unto the Lord;
With my voice unto the Lord do I make supplication.
    I pour out my complaint before him;
    I shew before him my trouble.
When my spirit was overwhelmed within me, thou knewest my path.
    In the way wherein I walk have they hidden a snare for me.
Look on my right hand, and see; for there is no man that knoweth me:
    Refuge hath failed me; no man careth for my soul.
I cried unto thee, O Lord;
I said, Thou art my refuge,
My portion in the land of the living.
    Attend unto my cry; for I am brought very low:
    Deliver me from my persecutors; for they are stronger than I.
Bring my soul out of prison, that I may give thanks unto thy name:
    The righteous shall compass me about;
    For thou shalt deal bountifully with me.

PSALM CXLIII.

Hear my prayer, O Lord; give ear to my supplications:
    In thy faithfulness answer me, and in thy righteousness.
And enter not into judgement with thy servant;
For in thy sight shall no man living be justified.
    I remember the days of old;
    I meditate on all thy doings:
I muse on the work of thy hands.
I spread forth my hands unto thee:
    My soul thirsteth after thee, as a weary land.
Make haste to answer me, O Lord; my spirit faileth:
    Hide not thy face from me;
    Lest I become like them that go down into the pit.
Cause me to hear thy lovingkindness in the morning;
For in thee do I trust:
    Cause me to know the way wherein I should walk;
    For I lift up my soul unto thee.
Deliver me, O Lord, from mine enemies:
I flee unto thee to hide me.
    Teach me to do thy will; for thou art my God:
    Thy spirit is good; lead me in the land of uprightness.
Quicken me, O Lord, for thy name's sake:
In thy righteousness bring my soul out of trouble.

PSALM CXLIV.

Lord, what is man, that thou takest knowledge of him?
    Or the son of man, that thou makest account of him?
Man is like to vanity:
His days are as a shadow that passeth away.

PSALM CXLV.

I will extol thee, my God, O King;
And I will bless thy name for ever and ever.
Every day will I bless thee;
And I will praise thy name for ever and ever.
Great is the Lord, and highly to be praised;
And his greatness is unsearchable.
One generation shall laud thy works to another,
And shall declare thy mighty acts.
Of the glorious majesty of thine honour,
And of thy wondrous works, will I meditate.
And men shall speak of the might of thy terrible acts;
And I will declare thy greatness.
They shall utter the memory of thy great goodness,
And shall sing of thy righteousness.
The Lord is gracious, and full of compassion;
Slow to anger, and of great mercy.
The Lord is good to all;
And his tender mercies are over all his works.
All thy works shall give thanks unto thee, O Lord;
And thy saints shall bless thee.
They shall speak of the glory of thy kingdom,
And talk of thy power;
To make known to the sons of men his mighty acts,
And the glory of the majesty of his kingdom.
Thy kingdom is an everlasting kingdom,
And thy dominion endureth throughout all generations.
The Lord upholdeth all that fall,
And raiseth up all those that be bowed down.
The eyes of all wait upon thee;
And thou givest them their meat in due season.
Thou openest thine hand,
And satisfiest the desire of every living thing.

The Lord is righteous in all his ways,
And gracious in all his works.
> The Lord is nigh unto all them that call upon him,
> To all that call upon him in truth.

He will fulfil the desire of them that fear him;
He also will hear their cry, and will save them.
> The Lord preserveth all them that love him;
> But all the wicked will he destroy.

My mouth shall speak the praise of the Lord:
> And let all flesh bless his holy name for ever and ever.

PSALM CXLVI.

Praise ye the Lord.
Praise the Lord, O my soul.
> While I live will I praise the Lord:
> I will sing praises unto my God while I have any being.

Put not your trust in princes,
Nor in the son of man, in whom there is no help.
> His breath goeth forth, he returneth to his earth;
> In that very day his thoughts perish.

Happy is he that hath the God of Jacob for his help,
Whose hope is in the Lord his God:
> Which made heaven and earth,
> The sea, and all that in them is;

Which keepeth truth for ever:
Which executeth judgement for the oppressed;
> Which giveth food to the hungry:
> The Lord looseth the prisoners;

The Lord openeth the eyes of the blind;
The Lord raiseth up them that are bowed down;
> The Lord loveth the righteous;
> The Lord preserveth the strangers;

He upholdeth the fatherless and widow;
But the way of the wicked he turneth upside down.
> The Lord shall reign for ever,
> Thy God, O Zion, unto all generations.

PRAISE YE THE LORD.

PSALM CXLVII.

Praise ye the Lord;
For it is good to sing praises unto our God;
> For it is pleasant, and praise is comely.

The Lord doth build up Jerusalem;
He gathereth together the outcasts of Israel.
> He healeth the broken in heart,
> And bindeth up their wounds.

He telleth the number of the stars;
He giveth them all their names.
> Great is our Lord, and mighty in power;
> His understanding is infinite.

The Lord upholdeth the meek:
He bringeth the wicked down to the ground.
> Sing unto the Lord with thanksgiving;
> Sing praises upon the harp unto our God:

Who covereth the heaven with clouds,
Who prepareth rain for the earth,
Who maketh grass to grow upon the mountains.
> He giveth to the beast his food,
> And to the young ravens which cry.

He delighteth not in the strength of the horse:
He taketh no pleasure in the legs of a man.
> The Lord taketh pleasure in them that fear him,
> In those that hope in his mercy.

Praise the Lord, O Jerusalem;
Praise thy God, O Zion.

For he hath strengthened the bars of thy gates;
He hath blessed thy children within thee.
He maketh peace in thy borders;
He filleth thee with the finest of the wheat.
> He sendeth out his commandment upon earth;
> His word runneth very swiftly.
He giveth snow like wool;
He scattereth the hoar frost like ashes.
> He casteth forth his ice like morsels:
> Who can stand before his cold?
He sendeth out his word, and melteth them:
He causeth his wind to blow, and the waters flow.
> He sheweth his word unto Jacob,
> His statutes and his judgements unto Israel.
He hath not dealt so with any nation:
And as for his judgements, they have not known them.
PRAISE YE THE LORD.

PSALM CXLVIII.

Praise ye the Lord.
> Praise ye the Lord from the heavens:
> Praise him in the heights.

Praise ye him, all his angels:
Praise ye him, all his host.
> Praise ye him, sun and moon:
> Praise him, all ye stars of light.

Praise him, ye heavens of heavens,
And ye waters that be above the heavens.
> Let them praise the name of the Lord:
> For he commanded, and they were created.

He hath also stablished them for ever and ever:
> He hath made a decree which shall not pass away.

Praise the Lord from the earth,
Ye dragons, and all deeps:
    Fire and hail, snow and vapour;
    Stormy wind, fulfilling his word:
Mountains and all hills;
Fruitful trees and all cedars:
    Beasts and all cattle;
    Creeping things and flying fowl:
Kings of the earth and all peoples;
Princes and all judges of the earth:
    Both young men and maidens;
    Old men and children:
Let them praise the name of the Lord;
For his name alone is exalted:
    His glory is above the earth and heaven.
And he hath lifted up the horn of his people,
The praise of all his saints;
Even of the children of Israel, a people near unto him.
PRAISE YE THE LORD.

PSALM CXLIX.

Praise ye the Lord.
    Sing unto the Lord a new song,
    And his praise in the assembly of the saints.
Let Israel rejoice in him that made him:
    Let the children of Zion be joyful in their King.
Let them praise his name in the dance:
    Let them sing praises unto him with the timbrel and harp.
For the Lord taketh pleasure in his people:
    He will beautify the meek with salvation.
Let the saints exult in glory:
Let them sing for joy upon their beds.
    Let the high praises of God be in their mouth.

PSALM CL.

Praise ye the Lord.
Praise God in his sanctuary:
> Praise him in the firmament of his power.
> Praise him for his mighty acts:

Praise him according to his excellent greatness.
Praise him with the sound of the trumpet:
> Praise him with the psaltery and harp.
> Praise him with the timbrel and dance:

Praise him with stringed instruments and the pipe.
Praise him upon the loud cymbals:
> Praise him upon the high sounding cymbals.

LET EVERY THING THAT HATH BREATH PRAISE THE LORD.
PRAISE YE THE LORD.

SELECTIONS.

The Birth of Jesus the Christ.

Behold, a king shall reign in righteousness,
  And princes shall rule in judgement.
And a man shall be as an hiding place from the wind, and a covert from the tempest;
  As rivers of water in a dry place, as the shadow of a great rock in a weary land.
Then judgement shall dwell in the wilderness,
  And righteousness shall abide in the fruitful field.
And the work of righteousness shall be peace;
  And the effect of righteousness quietness and confidence for ever.
The wilderness and the solitary place shall be glad;
  And the desert shall rejoice, and blossom as the rose.
It shall blossom abundantly, and rejoice even with joy and singing;
  The glory of Lebanon shall be given unto it, the excellency of Carmel and Sharon:
They shall see the glory of the Lord,
  The excellency of our God.
Then the eyes of the blind shall be opened, and the ears of the deaf shall be unstopped.
  Then shall the lame man leap as an hart, and the tongue of the dumb shall sing:
For in the wilderness shall waters break out, and streams in the desert.
  And the glowing sand shall become a pool, and the thirsty ground springs of water.

And an high way shall be there, and a way, and it shall be called The way of holiness;
> The unclean shall not pass over it; but it shall be for those: the wayfaring men, yea fools, shall not err therein.

No lion shall be there, nor shall any ravenous beast go up thereon, they shall not be found there;
> But the redeemed shall walk there: and the ransomed of the Lord shall return, and come with singing unto Zion;

And everlasting joy shall be upon their heads:
> They shall obtain gladness and joy, and sorrow and sighing shall flee away.

Comfort ye, comfort ye my people, saith your God.
> Speak ye comfortably to Jerusalem, and cry unto her, that her warfare is accomplished, that her iniquity is pardoned;

That she hath received of the Lord's hand double for all her sins.
> The voice of one that crieth, Prepare ye in the wilderness the way of the Lord,

Make straight in the desert a high way for our God.
> Every valley shall be exalted, and every mountain and hill shall be made low:

And the crooked shall be made straight, and the rough places plain:
> And the glory of the Lord shall be revealed, and all flesh shall see it together: for the mouth of the Lord hath spoken it.

O thou that tellest good tidings to Zion, get thee up into the high mountain;
> O thou that tellest good tidings to Jerusalem, lift up thy voice with strength;

Lift it up, be not afraid; say unto the cities of Judah, Behold, your God!
> Behold, the Lord God will come as a mighty one, and his arm shall rule for him:

Behold, his reward is with him, and his recompense before him.
He shall feed his flock like a shepherd, he shall gather the lambs in his arm, and carry them in his bosom, and shall gently lead those that give suck.
Sing unto the Lord a new song, and his praise from the end of the earth.
Sing, O heavens; and be joyful, O earth; and break forth into singing, O mountains:
For the Lord hath comforted his people,
And will have compassion upon his afflicted.
And the ransomed of the Lord shall return, and come with singing unto Zion; and everlasting joy shall be upon their heads:
They shall obtain gladness and joy, and sorrow and sighing shall flee away.
Blessed be the Lord, the God of Israel;
For he hath visited and wrought redemption for his people,
And hath raised up a horn of salvation for us in the house of his servant David,
Salvation from our enemies, and from the hand of all that hate us;
To show mercy towards our fathers, and to remember his holy covenant;
The oath which he sware unto Abraham our Father,
To grant unto us that we being delivered out of the hand of our enemies should serve him with fear,
In holiness and righteousness before him all our days.
Glory to God in the highest,
And on earth peace among men in whom he is well pleased.
Now lettest thou thy servant depart, O Lord, according to thy word, in peace;
For mine eyes have seen thy salvation, which thou hast prepared before the face of all peoples;

A light for revelation to the Gentiles, and the glory of thy people Israel.

Now unto the King eternal, incorruptible, invisible, the only God, be honour and glory for ever and ever.

AMEN.

[From the Prophecies of Isaiah and the Gospel according to Luke.]

THE RESURRECTION OF JESUS THE CHRIST.

But now hath Christ been raised from the dead, the first fruits of them that are asleep.

For since by man came death, by man came also the resurrection of the dead.

For as in Adam all die, so also in Christ shall all be made alive.

We shall not all sleep, but we shall all be changed, in a moment, in the twinkling of an eye, at the last trump:

For the trumpet shall sound, and the dead shall be raised incorruptible, and we shall be changed.

For this corruptible must put on incorruption, and this mortal must put on immortality.

But when this corruptible shall have put on incorruption, and this mortal shall have put on immortality, then shall come to pass the saying that is written, Death is swallowed up in victory.

O death, where is thy victory? O death, where is thy sting?

The sting of death is sin; and the power of sin is the law:

But thanks be to God, which giveth us the victory through our Lord Jesus Christ.

But having the same spirit of faith, according to that which is written, I believed, and therefore did I speak; we also believe, and therefore also we speak;

Knowing that he which raised up the Lord Jesus shall raise up us also with Jesus, and shall present us with you.

Wherefore we faint not; but though our outward man is decaying, yet our inward man is renewed day by day.

For our light affliction, which is for the moment, worketh for us more and more exceedingly an eternal weight of glory;

While we look not at the things which are seen, but at the things which are not seen:

For the things which are seen are temporal; but the things which are not seen are eternal.

For we know that if the earthly house of this tabernacle be dissolved, we have a building from God,

A house not made with hands, eternal, in the heavens.

For verily in this we groan, longing to be clothed upon with our habitation which is from heaven:

If so be that being clothed we shall not be found naked.

For indeed we that are in this tabernacle do groan, being burdened;

Not for that we would be unclothed, but that we would be clothed upon, that what is mortal may be swallowed up of life.

Now he that hath wrought us for this very thing is God,

Who gave unto us the earnest of the Spirit.

Being therefore always of good courage, and knowing that, whilst we are at home in the body, we are absent from the Lord; we are of good courage, I say,

And are willing rather to be absent from the body, and to be at home with the Lord.

Who shall lay anything to the charge of God's elect?

It is God that justifieth;

Who is he that shall condemn?

It is Christ Jesus that died, yea rather, that was raised from the dead, who is at the right hand of God, who also maketh intercession for us.

Who shall separate us from the love of Christ? shall tribulation, or anguish, or persecution, or famine, or nakedness, or peril, or sword?

Nay, in all these things we are more than conquerors through him that loved us.

For I am persuaded, that neither death, nor life, nor angels, nor principalities, nor things present, nor things to come, nor powers, nor height, nor depth, nor any other creature, shall be able to separate us from the love of God, which is in Christ Jesus our Lord.

Blessed be the God and Father of our Lord Jesus Christ, who according to his great mercy begat us again unto a living hope by the resurrection of Jesus Christ from the dead,

Unto an inheritance incorruptible, and undefiled, and that fadeth not away, reserved in heaven for you, who by the power of God are guarded through faith unto a salvation ready to be revealed in the last time.

Now unto him that is able to do exceeding abundantly above all that we ask or think, according to the power that worketh in us, unto him be the glory in the church and in Christ Jesus unto all generations for ever and ever.

Now our Lord Jesus Christ himself, and God our Father which loved us and gave us eternal comfort and good hope through grace, comfort your hearts and stablish them in every good work and word.

Worthy is the Lamb that hath been slain to receive the power, and riches, and wisdom, and might, and honour, and glory, and blessing.

Unto him that sitteth on the throne, and unto the Lamb, be the blessing, and the honour, and the glory, and the dominion, for ever and ever.

Amen.

[From I Corinthians, II Corinthians, Romans, I Peter, Ephesians, II Thessalonians, Revelation.]

The Work of Christian Missions.

O Lord, thou art my God; I will exalt thee,
>For thou hast done wonderful things, even counsels of old, in faithfulness and truth.

For thou hast been a strong hold to the poor, a strong hold to the needy in his distress,
>A refuge from the storm, a shadow from the heat, when the blast of the terrible ones is as a storm against the wall.

He hath swallowed up death for ever; and the Lord God will wipe away tears from off all faces;
>And the reproach of his people shall he take away from off all the earth: for the Lord hath spoken it.

And it shall be said in that day, Lo, this is our God; we have waited for him, and he will save us;
>This is the Lord; we have waited for him, we will be glad and rejoice in his salvation.

We have a strong city; salvation will he appoint for walls and bulwarks.
>Open ye the gates, that the righteous nation which keepeth truth may enter in.

Thou wilt keep him in perfect peace, whose mind is stayed on thee: because he trusteth in thee.
>Trust ye in the Lord for ever: for in the Lord Jehovah is an everlasting rock.

Lord, thou wilt ordain peace for us: for thou hast also wrought all our works for us.
>O Lord our God, other lords beside thee have had dominion over us; but by thee only will we make mention of thy name.

How beautiful upon the mountains are the feet of him that bringeth good tidings, that publisheth peace,
>That bringeth good tidings of good, that publisheth salvation;

That saith unto Zion, Thy God reigneth!
> The voice of thy watchmen! they lift up the voice, together do they sing;

For they shall see, eye to eye, when the Lord returneth to Zion.
> Break forth into joy, sing together, ye waste places of Jerusalem:

For the Lord hath comforted his people, he hath redeemed Jerusalem.
> The Lord hath made bare his holy arm in the eyes of all the nations;

And all the ends of the earth shall see the salvation of our God.
> Sing, O barren, thou that didst not bear; break forth into singing, and cry aloud,

For more are the children of the desolate than the children of the married wife, saith the Lord.
> Enlarge the place of thy tent, and let them stretch forth the curtains of thy habitations;

Spare not; lengthen thy cords, and strengthen thy stakes.
> For thou shalt spread abroad on the right hand and the left; and thy seed shall possess the nations.

Fear not; for thou shalt not be ashamed: neither be thou confounded; for thou shalt not be put to shame:
> For thou shalt forget the shame of thy youth, and the reproach of thy widowhood shalt thou remember no more.

For thy Maker is thine husband; the Lord of hosts is his name:
> And the Holy One of Israel is thy redeemer; the God of the whole earth shall he be called.

For a small moment have I forsaken thee; but with great mercies will I gather thee.
> In overflowing wrath I hid my face from thee for a moment; but with everlasting kindness will I have mercy on thee, saith the Lord thy redeemer.

And all thy children shall be taught of the Lord;
  And great shall be the peace of thy children.
Awake, awake, put on strength, O arm of the Lord;
  Awake, as in the days of old, the generations of ancient times.
Art thou not it which dried up the sea, the waters of the great deep;
  That made the depths of the sea a way for the redeemed to pass over?
And the ransomed of the Lord shall return, and come with singing unto Zion;
  And everlasting joy shall be upon their heads: they shall obtain gladness and joy, and sorrow and sighing shall flee away.

[From the Prophecies of Isaiah.]

The Work of Christian Missions.

And it shall come to pass in the latter days, that the mountain of the Lord's house shall be established in the top of the mountains, and shall be exalted above the hills;
  And all nations shall flow unto it.
And many peoples shall go and say, Come ye, and let us go up to the mountain of the Lord, to the house of the God of Jacob;
  And he will teach us of his ways, and we will walk in his paths:
For out of Zion shall go forth the law,
  And the word of the Lord from Jerusalem.
And he shall judge between the nations, and shall reprove many peoples:

And they shall beat their swords into ploughshares, and their
spears into pruning-hooks:
Nation shall not lift up sword against nation,
Neither shall they learn war any more.
In that day shall the branch of the Lord be beautiful and
glorious,
And the fruit of the land shall be excellent and comely for
them that are escaped of Israel.
For over all the glory shall be spread a canopy.
And there shall be a pavilion for a shadow in the day-time,
from the heat, and for a refuge and for a covert from the
storm and from rain.
The people that walked in darkness have seen a great light:
They that dwelt in the land of the shadow of death, upon
them hath the light shined.
Thou hast multiplied the nation, thou hast increased their
joy:
They joy before thee according to the joy in harvest, as men
rejoice when they divide the spoil.
For unto us a child is born, unto us a son is given; and the
government shall be upon his shoulder:
And his name shall be called Wonderful, Counsellor, Mighty
God, Everlasting Father, Prince of Peace.
Of the increase of his government and of peace there shall
be no end, upon the throne of David, and upon his
kingdom, to establish it,
And to uphold it with judgement and with righteousness
from henceforth even for ever.
And there shall come forth a shoot out of the stock of Jesse,
And a branch out of his roots shall bear fruit:
And the spirit of the Lord shall rest upon him, the spirit of
wisdom and understanding.
The spirit of counsel and might, the spirit of knowledge and
of the fear of the Lord;

And his delight shall be in the fear of the Lord:
 And he shall not judge after the sight of his eyes, neither reprove after the hearing of his ears:
But with righteousness shall he judge the poor, and reprove with equity for the meek of the earth.
 And righteousness shall be the girdle of his loins, and faithfulness the girdle of his reins.
And the wolf shall dwell with the lamb, and the leopard shall lie down with the kid;
 And the calf and the young lion and the fatling together; and a little child shall lead them.
And the cow and the bear shall feed; their young ones shall lie down together:
 And the lion shall eat straw like the ox.
They shall not hurt nor destroy in all my holy mountain:
 For the earth shall be full of the knowledge of the Lord, as the waters cover the sea.
And it shall come to pass in that day, that the root of Jesse, which standeth for an ensign of the peoples, unto him shall the nations seek;
 And his resting place shall be glorious.
And in that day thou shalt say, I will give thanks unto thee, O Lord.
 Behold, God is my salvation; I will trust, and will not be afraid:
For the Lord Jehovah is my strength and my song;
 And he is become my salvation.
Therefore with joy shall ye draw water out of the wells of salvation.
 Give thanks unto the Lord, call upon his name, declare his doings among the peoples, make mention that his name is exalted.
Sing unto the Lord; for he hath done excellent things:
 Let this be known in all the earth.

Cry aloud and shout, thou inhabitant of Zion:
: For great is the Holy One of Israel in the midst of thee.

[From the Prophecies of Isaiah.]

For a Public Day of Fasting.

I will make mention of the lovingkindnesses of the Lord, and the praises of the Lord, according to all that the Lord hath bestowed on us;
: And the great goodness toward the house of Israel, which he hath bestowed on them according to his mercies, and according to the multitude of his lovingkindnesses.

In all their affliction he was afflicted, and the angel of his presence saved them:
: In his love and in his pity he redeemed them; and he bare them, and carried them all the days of old.

But they rebelled and grieved his holy spirit:
: Therefore he was turned to be their enemy, and himself fought against them.

Then he remembered the days of old, Moses, and his people, saying, Where is he that brought them up out of the sea with the shepherds of his flock?
: Where is he that put his holy spirit in the midst of them? That caused his glorious arm to go at the right hand of Moses? that divided the water before them?

Look down from heaven, and behold from the habitation of thy holiness and of thy glory: where is thy zeal and thy mighty acts?
: The yearning of thy bowels and thy compassions are restrained toward me.

For thou art our father, though Abraham knoweth us not, and Israel doth not acknowledge us:

Thou, O Lord, art our father; our redeemer from everlasting is thy name.

Oh that thou wouldest rend the heavens, that thou wouldest come down,

For we are all become as one that is unclean, and all our righteousnesses are as a polluted garment:

And we all do fade as a leaf; and our iniquities, like the wind, take us away.

And there is none that calleth upon thy name, that stirreth up himself to take hold of thee:

For thou hast hid thy face from us, and hast consumed us by means of our iniquities.

But now, O Lord, thou art our father; we are the clay, and thou our potter; and we all are the work of thy hand.

Be not wroth very sore, O Lord, neither remember iniquity for ever:

Behold, look, we beseech thee, we are all thy people.

Though our iniquities testify against us, work thou for thy name's sake, O Lord:

For our backslidings are many; we have sinned against thee.

O thou hope of Israel, the saviour thereof in the time of trouble, why shouldst thou be a sojourner in the land,

And as a wayfaring man that turneth aside to tarry for a night?

Why shouldst thou be as a man astonied, as a mighty man that cannot save?

Yet thou, O Lord, art in the midst of us, and we are called by thy name; leave us not.

It is of the Lord's mercies that we are not consumed, because his compassions fail not.

They are new every morning; great is thy faithfulness.

The Lord is my portion, saith my soul; therefore will I hope in him.

The Lord is good unto them that wait for him, to the soul that seeketh him.
It is good that a man should hope and quietly wait for the salvation of the Lord.
For the Lord will not cast off for ever.
For though he cause grief, yet will he have compassion according to the multitude of his mercies.
For he doth not afflict willingly, nor grieve the children of men.
Wherefore doth a living man complain, a man for the punishment of his sins?
Let us search and try our ways, and turn again to the Lord.
Let us lift up our heart with our hands unto God in the heavens.
I called upon thy name, O Lord, out of the lowest dungeon.
Thou heardest my voice; hide not thine ear at my breathing, at my cry!
Thou, O Lord, abidest for ever;
Thy throne is from generation to generation.
Wherefore dost thou forget us for ever, and forsake us so long time?
Turn thou us unto thee, O Lord, and we shall be turned; renew our days as of old.
Though the fig tree shall not blossom,
Neither shall fruit be in the vines;
The labour of the olive shall fail,
And the fields shall yield no meat;
The flocks shall be cut off from the fold,
And there shall be no herd in the stalls:
Yet I will rejoice in the Lord,
I will joy in the God of my salvation.
Jehovah, the Lord, is my strength,
And he maketh my feet like hind's feet, and will make me to walk upon my high places.

[From Isaiah, Jeremiah, Lamentations, Habakkuk.]

THE LORD'S SUPPER.

Who hath believed our report?
And to whom hath the arm of the Lord been revealed?
> For he grew up before him as a tender plant, and as a root out of a dry ground:
> He hath no form nor comeliness; and when we see him, there is no beauty that we should desire him.

He was despised and rejected of men; a man of sorrows, and acquainted with grief:
And as one from whom men hide their face he was despised, and we esteemed him not.
> Surely he hath borne our griefs, and carried our sorrows:
> Yet we did esteem him stricken, smitten of God, and afflicted.

But he was wounded for our transgressions, he was bruised for our iniquities:
The chastisement of our peace was upon him; and with his stripes we are healed.
> All we like sheep have gone astray; we have turned every one to his own way;
> And the Lord hath laid on him the iniquity of us all.

He was oppressed, yet he humbled himself and opened not his mouth;
> As a lamb that is led to the slaughter, and as a sheep that before her shearers is dumb; yea, he opened not his mouth.

By oppression and judgement he was taken away;
> And as for his generation, who among them considered that he was cut off out of the land of the living?

For the transgression of my people was he stricken.
> And they made his grave with the wicked, and with the rich in his death;

Although he had done no violence, neither was any deceit in his mouth.
> Yet it pleased the Lord to bruise him; he hath put him to grief:

When thou shalt make his soul an offering for sin, he shall
  see his seed, he shall prolong his days,
And the pleasure of the Lord shall prosper in his hand.
  He shall see of the travail of his soul, and shall be satisfied:
By his knowledge shall my righteous servant justify many:
  and he shall bear their iniquities.
Therefore will I divide him a portion with the great, and he
  shall divide the spoil with the strong;
  Because he poured out his soul unto death, and was numbered
    with the transgressors:
  Yet he bare the sins of many,
  And made intercession for the transgressors.
Ho, every one that thirsteth, come ye to the waters, and he
  that hath no money; come ye, buy, and eat;
Yea, come, buy wine and milk without money and without
  price.
  Wherefore do ye spend money for that which is not bread?
  And your labour for that which satisfieth not?
Hearken diligently unto me, and eat ye that which is good,
  and let your soul delight itself in fatness.
Incline your ear, and come unto me; hear, and your soul
  shall live.
  Seek ye the Lord while he may be found,
  Call ye upon him while he is near:
Let the wicked forsake his way, and the unrighteous man
  his thoughts: and let him return unto the Lord, and
  he will have mercy upon him;
And to our God, for he will abundantly pardon.
  For my thoughts are not your thoughts,
  Neither are your ways my ways, saith the Lord.
For as the heavens are higher than the earth, so are my ways
  higher than your ways,
  And my thoughts than your thoughts.

For as the rain cometh down and the snow from heaven, and returneth not thither, but watereth the earth, and maketh it bring forth and bud, and giveth seed to the sower and bread to the eater;
So shall my word be that goeth forth out of my mouth:
It shall not return unto me void, but it shall accomplish that which I please,
And it shall prosper in the thing whereto I sent it.
For ye shall go out with joy,
And be led forth with peace:
The mountains and the hills shall break forth before you into singing,
And all the trees of the fields shall clap their hands.
Instead of the thorn shall come up the fir tree, and instead of the briar shall come up the myrtle tree:
And it shall be to the Lord for a name, for an everlasting sign that shall not be cut off.

Service for the Dedication of a Church.

O Lord, the God of Israel, there is no God like thee, in heaven above, or on earth beneath;
Who keepest covenant and mercy with thy servants, that walk before thee with all their heart.
But will God in very deed dwell on the earth? Behold, heaven and the heaven of heavens cannot contain thee;
How much less this house that we have builded.
Yet have thou respect unto the prayer of thy servant, and to his supplication, O Lord my God,
That thine eyes may be open toward this house night and day, even toward the place whereof thou hast said, My name shall be there.

And hearken thou to the supplication of thy servant, and of thy people Israel, when they shall pray toward this place:
  Yea, hear thou in heaven thy dwelling place; and when thou hearest, forgive.
The Lord our God be with us, as he was with our fathers: let him not leave us, nor forsake us:
  That he may incline our hearts unto him, to walk in all his ways, and to keep his commandments, and his statutes, and his judgements, which he commanded our fathers.
Arise, O Lord God, into thy resting place,
  Thou, and the ark of thy strength:
Let thy priests, O Lord God, be clothed with salvation,
  And let thy saints rejoice in goodness.
For the Lord hath chosen Zion; he hath desired it for his habitation.
  This is my resting place for ever: here will I dwell; for I have desired it.
I will abundantly bless her provision: I will satisfy her poor with bread.
  Her priests also will I clothe with salvation: and her saints shall shout aloud for joy.
Behold, bless ye the Lord, all ye servants of the Lord, lift up your hands to the sanctuary, and bless ye the Lord.
  The Lord bless thee out of Zion; even he that made heaven and earth.
Praise ye the Lord, ye that stand in the house of the Lord.
  Sing praises unto his name; for it is pleasant.
Sing unto the Lord a new song, and his praise in the assembly of the saints.
  Let Israel rejoice in him that made him: let the children of Zion be joyful in their King.

I will pay my vows unto the Lord, in the courts of the Lord's house.

Open to me the gates of righteousness: I will enter into them, I will give thanks unto the Lord.

This is the gate of the Lord; the righteous shall enter into it.

I will give thanks unto thee, for thou hast answered me, and art become my salvation.

The stone which the builders rejected is become the head of the corner.

This is the Lord's doing; it is marvellous in our eyes.

Blessed be he that cometh in the name of the Lord:

We have blessed you out of the house of the Lord.

Thou art my God, and I will give thanks unto thee: thou art my God, I will exalt thee.

O give thanks unto the Lord; for he is good: for his mercy endureth for ever.

A Morning Service.

FOR THE USE OF

CONGREGATIONS, COLLEGES, SCHOOLS, AND ACADEMIES, FOR SUNDAY MORNING WORSHIP.

BY THE
Rev. JOSEPH T. DURYEA, D.D.

BOSTON AND CHICAGO:
Congregational Sunday-School and Publishing Society.

COPYRIGHT, 1888, BY
CONGREGATIONAL SUNDAY-SCHOOL AND PUBLISHING SOCIETY.

THIS MORNING SERVICE is meant to be suggestive rather than arbitrary. It contains features which have commended themselves by use in various prominent churches. They are here given for such adoption as the circumstances of each case may indicate as advantageous and wise.

A Morning Service.

Voluntary.

A sentence from the Scripture. (One or more read by the minister or sung.)

The Lord is in his holy temple: let all the earth keep silence before him.

O worship the Lord in the beauty of holiness. . . . Enter into his gates with thanksgiving, and into his courts with praise.

It is a good thing to give thanks unto the Lord, and to sing praises unto his name.

O come, let us worship and bow down: let us kneel before the Lord our maker.

Sing unto the Lord, bless his name; shew forth his salvation from day to day.

What shall I render unto the Lord for all his benefits toward me? I will take the cup of salvation, and call upon the name of the Lord. I will pay my vows unto the Lord now in the presence of all his people.

The Lord will command his lovingkindness in the daytime, and in the night his song shall be with me, and my prayer unto the God of my life.

Seek ye the Lord while he may be found, call ye upon him while he is near.

Let us lift up our heart with our hands unto God in the heavens.

Hear ye the word of the Lord . . . incline your ears to the word of his mouth.

I will hear what God the Lord will speak: for he will speak peace unto his people.

A MORNING SERVICE.

Doxology. (Congregation standing.)

Praise God, from whom all blessings flow! Praise him, all creatures here be-low!
Praise him a-bove, ye heaven-ly host! Praise Father, Son, and Ho-ly Ghost.

Invocation. (Congregation standing.)

ALL. — Almighty God, unto whom all hearts are open, all desires known, and from whom no secrets are hid; Cleanse the thoughts of our hearts by the inspiration of thy Holy Spirit, that we may perfectly love thee and worthily magnify thy holy name; through Jesus Christ our Lord: Who hath taught us when we pray to say: —

Our Father which art in heaven, Hallowed be thy name. Thy kingdom come. Thy will be done in earth, as it is in heaven. Give us this day our daily bread. And forgive us our debts, as we forgive our debtors. And lead us not into temptation, but deliver us from evil: For thine is the kingdom, and the power, and the glory, for ever. Amen.

Salutation; (optional) by the Minister (congregation still standing).

May Grace, Mercy, and Peace, from God the Father and Christ Jesus our Lord, be upon you all. Amen.

(Or some other form chosen by the Minister.)

A MORNING SERVICE.

Anthem. (By the Choir, at the option of the Minister.)

The Confession. (Congregation seated and bowing down.)

ALL. — Almighty and most merciful Father; We have erred and strayed from thy ways like lost sheep. We have followed too much the devices and desires of our own hearts. We have offended against thy holy laws. We have left undone those things which we ought to have done; and we have done those things which we ought not to have done; and there is no health in us. But thou, O Lord, have mercy upon us, miserable offenders. Spare thou those, O Lord, who confess their faults. Restore thou those who are penitent; according to thy promises declared unto mankind in Christ Jesus our Lord. And grant, O most merciful Father, for his sake; that we may hereafter live a godly, righteous, and sober life, to the glory of thy holy name. Amen.

[OR THIS.]

Almighty God, Father of our Lord Jesus Christ, Maker of all things, Judge of all men; We acknowledge and bewail our manifold sins and wickedness, which we, from time to time, most grievously have committed, by thought, word, and deed, against thy Divine Majesty, provoking most justly thy wrath and indignation against us. We do earnestly repent, and are heartily sorry for these our misdoings; the remembrance of them is grievous unto us; the burden of them is intolerable. Have mercy upon us, have mercy upon us, most merciful Father; for thy Son our Lord Jesus Christ's sake, forgive us all that is past; and grant that we may ever hereafter serve and please thee in newness of life, to the honor and glory of thy name; through Jesus Christ our Lord. Amen.

Hymn. (Congregation standing.)

Scripture Lesson. (Congregation seated.)

A MORNING SERVICE. 5

[If preferred, these selections may be *read* by the minister and people alternately]

Chant. A. R. REINAGLE.

PSALM XCV.

1. O come, let us *sing* | unto · the | Lord ‖ let us make a joyful *noise* to the | Rock · of | our · sal | vation.

2. Let us come before his *presence* with | thanks · — | giving ‖ and make a joyful *noise* | un · to | him · with | psalms.

3. For the *Lord* is a | great · — | God ‖ and a great *King* | above · — | all · — | gods.

4. In his hand are the deep *places* | of · the | earth ‖ the *strength* of the | hills · is | his · — | also.

5. The sea is *his* and | he · — | made it ‖ and his *hands* | formed · the | dry · — | land.

6. O come, let us *worship* and | bow · — | down ‖ let us *kneel* be- | fore · the | Lord · our | maker.

7. For *he* | is · our | God ‖ and we are the people of his pasture *and* the | sheep · of | his · — | hand.

8. O worship the *Lord* in the | beauty of | holiness ‖ *fear* be | fore · him | all the | earth.

9. Let the heavens rejoice, and *let* the | earth · be | glad ‖ let the sea *roar* and the | ful · ness | there · — | of.

10. Let the field be joyful, and *all* that | is · there | in ‖ then shall *all* the | trees · of the | wood · re | joice.

11. Before the Lord : for he cometh, for he *cometh* to | judge · the | earth ‖ he shall judge the world with righteous*ness* and the | peo · ple | with · his | truth.

Glory be to the *Father* | and · to the | Son ‖ *and* | to · the | Ho · ly | Ghost.

As it was in the beginning, is *now* and | ev · er | shall be ‖ *World* without | end · — | A · — | men.

A MORNING SERVICE.

[OR THIS.] ANON.

A - MEN.

1. We praise thee, | O— | God; ‖ we acknowledge | thee to | be the | Lord. ‖ All the earth doth | worship | thee. ‖ the Father | ever- | last- — | ing. ‖

2. To thee all angels | cry a- | loud, ‖ the heavens, and | all the | powers there- | in. To thee cherubim and seraphim, con- | tinually ·· do | cry, ‖ Holy, holy, holy, Lord | God of | Saba- | oth; ‖

3. Heaven and earth are full of the majesty | of thy | glory. ‖ The glorious company of the apostles praise thee. The goodly fellowship of the | prophets | praise — | thee. ‖ The noble army of martyrs | praise — | thee. ‖ The holy church throughout all the | world ·· doth ac- | knowledge | thee, ‖

4. The Father, of an | infi- ·· nite | majesty; ‖ thine adorable, | true and | only | Son; ‖ Also the Holy | Ghost, the | Comforter. ‖ Thou art the King of glory, O Christ, thou art the everlasting | Son ·· of the | Fa- — | ther. ‖

5. When thou tookest upon thee to de- | liver | man, ‖ thou didst humble thyself to be | born — | of a | virgin. ‖ When thou hadst overcome the | sharpness ·· of | death, ‖ thou didst open the kingdom of | heaven ·· to | all be- | lievers. ‖

6. Thou sittest at the right hand of God, in the | glory ·· of the | Father. ‖ We believe that thou shalt | come to | be our | judge. We therefore pray thee, | help thy | servants, ‖ whom thou hast redeemed | with thy | precious | blood. ‖

A MORNING SERVICE. 7

7. Make them to be numbered | with thy | saints, || in | glory | ever- | lasting. || O Lord, save thy people, and | bless thine | heritage; || govern them and | lift them | up for- | ever. ||

8. Day by day we | magni-··fy | thee; || and we worship thy name ever, | world with- | out — | end. || Vouchsafe, O Lord, to keep us this | day with-out | sin; || O Lord, have mer-cy upon us, have | mer-cy up- | on — | us. ||

9. O Lord, let thy mercy | be up- | on us, || as our | trust — | is in | thee. || O Lord, in | thee·· have I | trusted; || let me | never | be con- | founded. || A- | men. ||

[OR THIS.]

R. N. PARKE.

PSALM XLVII.

1. God be merciful unto *us* and | bless·— | us || and *cause* his | face· to | shine·up | on us.

2. That thy way may be *known* up | on·— | earth || thy *saving* | health·a | mong·all | nations.

3. Let the people *praise* thee | O·— | God || *let* | all·the | peo··ple | praise thee.

4. O let the nations be *glad* and | sing·for | joy || for thou shalt judge the people righteously, and *gov*ern the | nations·up | on·— | earth.

5. Let the people *praise* thee | O·— | God || *let* | all·the | peo·ple | praise thee.

6. Then shall the *earth* | yield·her | increase || and God, even our own *God* | shall·— | bless·— | us.

7. *God* | shall·— | bless us || and all the *ends* of the | earth·shall | fear·— | him.

Glory be to the *Father* | and·to the | Son || *and* | to·the | Ho·ly | Ghost.

As it was in the beginning, is *now* and ev·er | shall be || *World* with-out end·— | A·— | men.

8   A MORNING SERVICE.

[OR THIS.]   BURROWES.

PSALM LXVII.

1. O sing unto the *Lord* a | new · — | song ‖ for *he* hath | done · — | marvel · lous | things.
2. His right *hand* and his | ho · ly | arm ‖ *hath* | got · ten | him · the | victory.
3. The Lord hath made *known* | his · sal | vation ‖ his righteousness hath he openly *shew*ed in the | sight · — | of · the | heathen.
4. He hath remembered his mercy and his truth *toward* the | house · of | Israel ‖ all the ends of the earth have *seen* the sal | va · tion | of · our | God.
5. Make a joyful noise unto the *Lord* | all · the | earth ‖ make a loud *noise* and re | joice · and | sing · — | praise.
6. Sing unto the *Lord* | with · the | harp ‖ with the *harp* | and · the | voice · of a | psalm.
7. With *trum*pets and | sound · of | cornet ‖ make a joyful *noise* be | fore · the | Lord · the | King.
8. Let the sea *roar* and the | fulness · there | of ‖ the *world* and | they · that | dwell · there | in.
9. Let the *floods* | clap · their | hands ‖ *let* the | hills · be | joyful · to | gether.
10. Before the Lord; for he *com*eth to | judge · the | earth · ‖ with righteousness shall he judge the *world* and the | peo · ple | with · — | equity.   J. HINDLE.

[OR THIS FOR OCCASIONAL USE.]

The Commandments. (Congregation seated and bowing down.)

[The Minister shall repeat the commandments, and the people, after each commandment, shall sing or repeat the appropriate response.]

MINISTER.— And God spake all these words, saying,
1. Thou shalt have no other gods before me.

A MORNING SERVICE.

Response (I-IX).

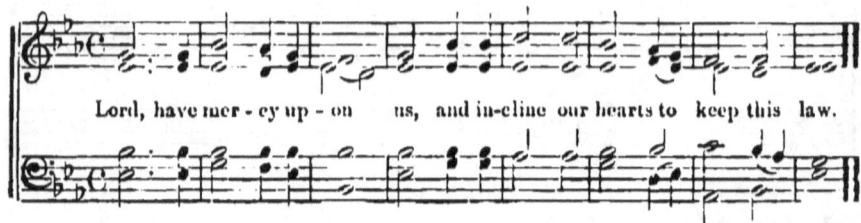

Lord, have mer-cy up-on us, and in-cline our hearts to keep this law.

II. Thou shalt not make unto thee any graven image, or any likeness of any thing that is in heaven above, or that is in the earth beneath, or that is in the water under the earth: thou shalt not bow down thyself to them, nor serve them: for I the Lord thy God am a jealous God, visiting the iniquity of the fathers upon the children unto the third and fourth generation of them that hate me; and shewing mercy unto thousands of them that love me, and keep my commandments.

Response. Lord, have mercy upon us, and incline our hearts to keep this law.

III. Thou shalt not take the name of the Lord thy God in vain; for the Lord will not hold him guiltless that taketh his name in vain.

Response. Lord, have mercy upon us, and incline our hearts to keep this law.

IV. Remember the sabbath day, to keep it holy. Six days shalt thou labour, and do all thy work: but the seventh day is the sabbath of the Lord thy God: in it thou shalt not do any work, thou, nor thy son, nor thy daughter, thy manservant, nor thy maidservant, nor thy cattle, nor thy stranger that is within thy gates: for in six days the Lord made heaven and earth, the sea, and all that in them is, and rested the seventh day: wherefore the Lord blessed the sabbath day, and hallowed it.

Response. Lord, have mercy upon us, and incline our hearts to keep this law.

V. Honour thy father and thy mother: that thy days may be long upon the land which the Lord thy God giveth thee.

Response. Lord, have mercy upon us, and incline our hearts to keep this law.

VI. Thou shalt not kill.

Response. Lord, have mercy upon us, and incline our hearts to keep this law.

VII. Thou shalt not commit adultery.

Response. Lord, have mercy upon us, and incline our hearts to keep this law.

VIII. Thou shalt not steal.

Response. Lord, have mercy upon us, and incline our hearts to keep this law.

IX. Thou shalt not bear false witness against thy neighbour.

Response. Lord, have mercy upon us, and incline our hearts to keep this law.

X. Thou shalt not covet thy neighbour's house, thou shalt not covet thy neighbour's wife, nor his manservant, nor his maidservant, nor his ox, nor his ass, nor any thing that is thy neighbour's.

Response.

Lord, have mer-cy up-on... us, and write all these thy laws in our hearts, we be-seech thee.

MINISTER. — Hear also what our Lord Jesus Christ saith: Thou shalt love the Lord thy God with all thy heart, and with all thy soul, and with all thy mind. This is the first and great commandment. And the second is like unto it: Thou shalt love thy neighbour as thyself. On these two commandments hang all the law and the prophets.

[*A brief prayer may follow the commandments, in this form if desired.*]

O Almighty Lord, and everlasting God, vouchsafe, we beseech thee, to direct, sanctify, and govern both our hearts and bodies in the way of thy laws, and in the works of thy commandments; that, through thy most mighty protection, both here and ever, we may be preserved in body and soul: through our Lord and Saviour, Jesus Christ. Amen.

A Selection from the Psalter.

(Read responsively by minister and people, all standing.)

Gloria Patri. (Congregation still standing.)

No. 1.   J. BARNBY.

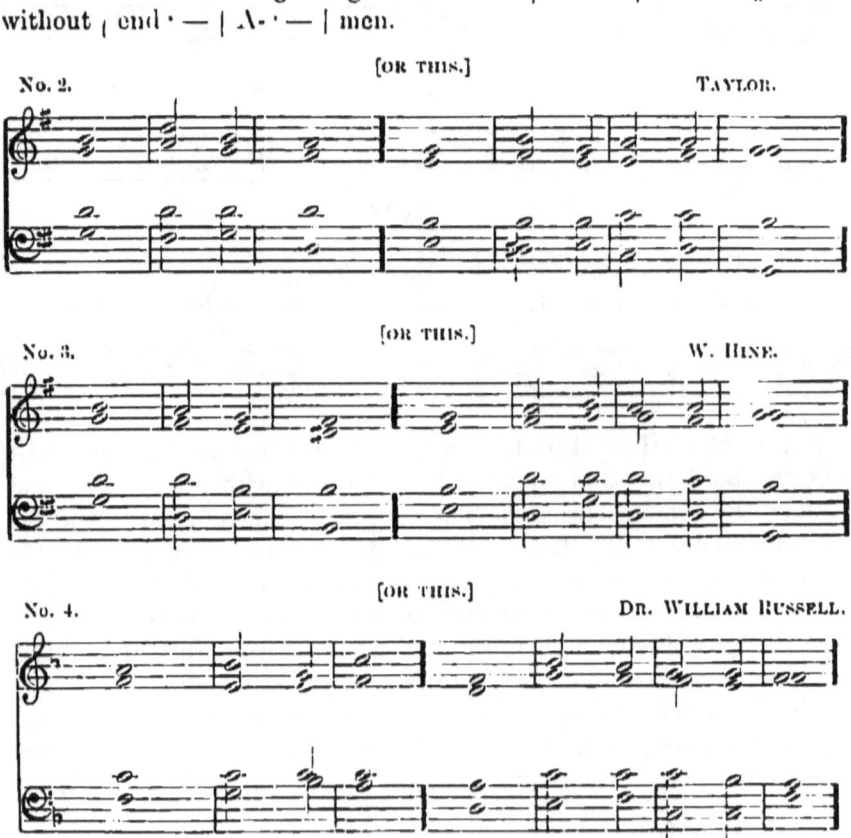

Glory be to the *Father* | and · to the | Son ‖ *and* | to · the | Holy | Ghost.

As it was in the beginning, is *now* and | ev- · er | shall be ‖ *World* without ǀ end · — | A- · — | men.

[OR THIS.]

No. 2.   TAYLOR.

[OR THIS.]

No. 3.   W. HINE.

[OR THIS.]

No. 4.   DR. WILLIAM RUSSELL.

The Apostles' Creed.   (Minister and congregation, all still standing.)

I believe in God the Father Almighty, Maker of heaven and earth; and in Jesus Christ, his only Son our Lord, who was conceived by the Holy Ghost, born of the Virgin Mary, suffered under Pontius Pilate, was crucified, dead, and buried; he descended into hell; the third day he rose from the dead; he ascended into heaven, and sitteth on the right hand of God the Father Almighty; from thence he shall come to judge the quick and the dead. I believe in the Holy Ghost; the Holy Catholic Church, the communion of saints; the forgiveness of sins; the resurrection of the body, and the life everlasting. Amen.

The Pastoral Prayer.   (Congregation bowing down.)

Offering and Announcements.

Hymn.   (Congregation standing.)

Sermon.

Anthem.   (At the option of the Minister.)

Hymn.   (Congregation standing.)

Prayer.   (Congregation seated and bowing down.)

[If desirable, in the use of any of the following.]

Grant, we beseech thee, Almighty God, that the words which we have heard this day with our outward ears may, through thy grace, be so grafted inwardly in our hearts, that they may bring forth in us the fruit of good living; to the honor and praise of thy name: Through Jesus Christ our Lord. Amen.

O Almighty God! who alone canst order the unruly wills and affections of sinful men: Grant unto us thy people, that we may love the things which thou commandest, and desire that which thou dost promise; that so, among the sundry and manifold changes of the world, our hearts may surely there be fixed, where true joys are to be found: Through Jesus Christ our Lord. Amen.

O God, Holy Ghost, Sanctifier of the faithful, visit, we pray thee, this congregation with thy love and favor; enlighten their minds more and more with the light of the everlasting gospel; graft in their hearts a love of the truth; increase in them true religion; nourish them with all goodness; and of thy great mercy keep them in the same, O Blessed Spirit: Whom, with the Father and the Son, together, we worship and glorify as one God, world without end. Amen.

Almighty God, who hast given us grace at this time with one accord to make our common supplications unto thee, and dost promise that when two or three are gathered together in thy name, thou wilt grant their requests: Fulfil now, O Lord, the desires and petitions of thy servants, as may be most expedient for them; granting us in this world knowledge of thy truth, and in the world to come life everlasting. Amen.

Benediction. (Congregation still seated and bowing down.)

The grace of the Lord Jesus Christ, and the love of God, and the communion of the Holy Ghost, be with you all.

[OR OTHER FORM TO BE CHOSEN BY THE MINISTER.]

Response. (By the Choir.)

[If the Minister will begin promptly, and the organist will omit interludes, this order will occupy one hour and thirty minutes. The organ prelude should begin five minutes before the hour of service and end on the minute.]

VESPER SERVICES.

FOR THE USE OF

CONGREGATIONS, COLLEGES, SCHOOLS, AND ACADEMIES,

FOR SUNDAY EVENING WORSHIP.

EDITED BY

REV. JOSEPH T. DURYEA, D.D.

BOSTON AND CHICAGO:
Congregational Sunday-School and Publishing Society.

Copyright, 1887, by
CONGREGATIONAL SUNDAY-SCHOOL AND PUBLISHING SOCIETY.

*Electrotyped and Printed by Stanley & Usher,
171 Devonshire Street, Boston.*

CONTENTS.

Vesper Service No. 1 . . . . .
Vesper Service No. 2 . . . .
Vesper Service No. 3 . . . . .
Vesper Service No. 4 . . . .
Vesper Service No. 5 . . . .

VESPER SERVICE.

No. 1.

———•———

[The congregation standing.]

MINISTER. — The Lord is in his holy temple: let all the earth keep silence before him.
PEOPLE. — Surely the Lord is in this place. This is none other but the house of God, and this is the gate of heaven.
The sacrifices of God are a broken spirit: a broken and a contrite heart, O God, thou wilt not despise.
Let the words of my mouth, and the meditation of my heart be acceptable in thy sight, O Lord, my strength and my redeemer.

Let us pray. (All uniting.)

Almighty God, unto whom all hearts are open, all desires known, and from whom no secrets are hid; cleanse the thoughts of our hearts by the inspiration of thy Holy Spirit, that we may perfectly love thee, and worthily magnify thy holy name; through Christ our Lord. Amen.

Our Father which art in heaven, hallowed be thy name. Thy kingdom come. Thy will be done on earth, as it is in heaven. Give us this day our daily bread. And forgive us our debts, as we forgive our debtors. And lead us not into temptation; but deliver us from evil: for thine is the kingdom, and the power, and the glory, for ever and ever. Amen.

VESPER SERVICE.

O DAY OF REST AND GLADNESS!

AURELIA.

1. O day of rest and gladness! O day of joy and light! O balm of care and sadness, Most beautiful, most bright! On thee, the high and lowly, Bending before the throne, Sing Holy, Holy, Holy, To the great Three in One!

On Thee, at the creation,
   The light first had its birth;
On Thee, for our salvation,
   Christ rose from depths of earth;
On Thee, our Lord, victorious,
   The Spirit sent from heaven,
And thus on Thee, most glorious,
   A triple light was given.

To-day on weary nations
　The heavenly manna falls;
To holy convocations
　The silver trumpet calls,
Where gospel light is glowing
　With pure and radiant beams,
And living water flowing
　With soul-refreshing streams.

New graces ever gaining
　From this our day of rest,
We reach the rest remaining
　To spirits of the blest:
To Holy Ghost be praises,
　To Father and to Son;
The Church her voice upraises
　To Thee, blest Three in One.

A - men.

[The congregation seated.]

Our Lord Jesus Christ saith: The first of all the commandments is, Hear, O Israel; the Lord our God is one Lord:

And thou shalt love the Lord thy God with all thy heart, and with all thy soul, and with all thy mind, and with all thy strength.

This is the first commandment. And the second is like, namely, this: Thou shalt love thy neighbour as thyself.

On these two commandments hang all the Law and the Prophets.

Teach me, O Lord, the way of thy statutes, and I shall keep it unto the end.

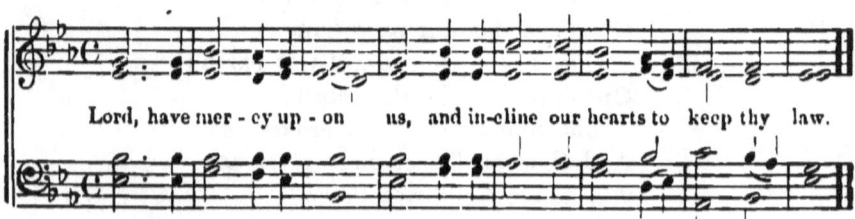

Lord, have mer - cy up - on us, and in-cline our hearts to keep thy law.

The Apostles' Creed.

(Recited in unison.)

I BELIEVE in God, the Father Almighty, Maker of heaven and earth; and in Jesus Christ, his only Son, our Lord; who was conceived by the Holy Ghost; born of the Virgin Mary; suffered under Pontius Pilate; was crucified, dead, and buried; he descended into hell. The third day he rose from the dead; he ascended into heaven, and sitteth at the right hand of God, the Father Almighty; from thence he shall come to judge the quick and the dead. A - men.

I believe in the Holy Ghost; the holy, catholic Church, the Communion of Saints; the Forgiveness of sins; the Resurrection of the body; and the Life everlasting.

Let us pray.

[Prayer by the Minister.]

GOD GREATER THAN OUR HEARTS.

1. Searcher of hearts! from mine e - rase All tho'ts that should not be, And in its deep re - cess - es trace My grat - i - tude to thee!

Hearer of prayer! Oh, guide aright
　Each word and deed of mine;
Life's battle teach me how to fight,
　And be the victory Thine.

Father, and Son, and Holy Ghost!
　Thou glorious Three in One!
Thou knowest best what I need most,
　And let Thy will be done.

A - men.

Responsive Reading.

[Congregation standing.]

How amiable are thy tabernacles,
O Lord of Hosts!
　My soul longeth, yea, even fainteth for the courts of the Lord;
My heart and my flesh cry out unto the living God.
　Yea, the sparrow hath found her an house,
　And the swallow a nest for herself, where she may lay her young,
Even thine altars, O Lord of hosts,
My King, and my God.
　Blessed are they that dwell in thy house:
　They will be still praising thee.
Blessed is the man whose strength is in thee;
In whose heart are the high ways to Zion.
Passing through the valley of Weeping they make it a place of springs;
　Yea, the early rain covereth it with blessings.
They go from strength to strength,
　Every one of them appeareth before God in Zion.
O Lord God of hosts, hear my prayer:
　Give ear, O God of Jacob.
Behold, O God our shield,
And look upon the face of thine anointed.

For a day in thy courts is better than a thousand.
I had rather be a doorkeeper in the house of my God,
Than to dwell in the tents of wickedness.
For the Lord God is a sun and a shield:
The Lord will give grace and glory:
No good thing will he withhold from them that walk uprightly.
O LORD OF HOSTS,
BLESSED IS THE MAN THAT TRUSTETH IN THEE.

GLORIA PATRI.

Glo - ry be to the Fa - ther, and to the Son, and to the Ho - ly Ghost; As it was in the be - gin - ning, is now and ev - er shall be, world with - out end. A - men. A - men.

[Congregation seated.]

Scripture Lesson.

Anthem.

Address or Sermon.

Prayer.

Responsive Reading.

Hear my cry, O God;
Attend unto my prayer.
    From the end of the earth will I call unto thee, when my heart is overwhelmed:
Lead me to the rock that is higher than I.
    For thou hast been a refuge for me,
    A strong tower from the enemy.
I will dwell in thy tabernacle for ever:
    I will take refuge in the covert of thy wings.
For thou, O God, hast heard my vows:
    Thou hast given me the heritage of those that fear thy name.
My soul waiteth only upon God:
From him cometh my salvation.
    He only is my rock and my salvation:
    He is my high tower; I shall not be greatly moved.
My soul, wait thou only upon God;
    For my expectation is from him.
He only is my rock and my salvation:
    He is my high tower; I shall not be moved.
With God is my salvation and my glory:
    The rock of my strength, and my refuge, is in God.
Trust in him at all times, ye people;
Pour out your heart before him:
    God is a refuge for us.

Surely men of low degree are vanity, and men of high degree are a lie:
    In the balances they will go up;
    They are together lighter than vanity.
Trust not in oppression,
And become not vain in robbery:
    If riches increase, set not your heart thereon.
God hath spoken once,
Twice have I heard this;
That power belongeth unto God:
    Also unto thee, O Lord, belongeth mercy:
    For thou renderest to every man according to his work.
O God, thou art my God; early will I seek thee:
    My soul thirsteth for thee, my flesh longeth for thee,
    In a dry and dreary land, where no water is.
So have I looked upon thee in the sanctuary,
To see thy power and thy glory.
    For thy lovingkindness is better than life;
    My lips shall praise thee.
So will I bless thee while I live:
    I will lift up my hands in thy name.
My soul shall be satisfied as with marrow and fatness;
And my mouth shall praise thee with joyful lips;
    When I remember thee upon my bed,
    And meditate on thee in the night watches.
For thou hast been my help,
And in the shadow of thy wings will I rejoice.
    My soul followeth hard after thee:
    Thy right hand upholdeth me.

A SONG IN THE NIGHT.

1. Now God be with us, for the night is clos-ing. Dark-ness and light are both of his dis-pos-ing. Be-neath his sha-dow, here to rest we yield us, For he will shield us.

Let evil thoughts and spirits flee before us;
Till morning cometh, watch, O Master, o'er us;
In soul and body Thou from harm defend us;
    Thine angels send us.

We have no refuge; none on earth to aid us,
Save Thee, O Father, who Thine own hast made us:
But Thy dear presence will not leave them lonely
    Who seek Thee only.

Father, Thy name be praised, Thy kingdom given,
Thy will be done on earth, as 't is in heaven;
Keep us in life, forgive our sins, deliver
    Us now and ever.

A - men.

VESPER SERVICE.

Let us pray. (Minister.)

O Lord, our heavenly Father, by whose almighty power we have been preserved this day; by thy great mercy defend us from all perils and dangers of this night; for the love of thy only Son, our Saviour, Jesus Christ.

Amen. (People.)

NOW THE DAY IS OVER.

[The Choir. All heads bowed.]

1. Now the day is o-ver, Night is draw-ing nigh, Sha-dows of the eve-ning Steal a-cross the sky. A-men.

Now the darkness gathers,
　Stars begin to peep;
Birds, and beasts, and flowers
　Soon will be asleep.

Jesus, give the weary
　Calm and sweet repose,
With Thy tend'rest blessing
　May our eyelids close.

VESPER SERVICE.

Grant to little children
   Visions bright of Thee,
Guard the sailors, tossing
   On the deep blue sea.

Comfort every sufferer
   Watching late in pain;
Those who plan some evil
   From their sin restrain.

Through the long night-watches,
   May Thine angels spread
Their white wings above me,
   Watching round my bed.

When the morning wakens,
   Then may I arise
Pure, and fresh, and sinless,
   In Thy holy eyes. Amen.

Benediction.

The Lord bless you and keep you:

The Lord make his face to shine upon you, and be gracious unto you:

The Lord lift up his countenance upon you, and give you peace.

The grace of our Lord Jesus Christ be with you.

Response.

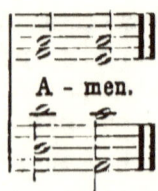

Vesper Service.

No. 2.

MINISTER. — It is a good thing to give thanks unto the Lord,
PEOPLE. — And to sing praises unto thy name, O Most High.
To shew forth thy lovingkindness in the morning,
And thy faithfulness every night.
O come, let us sing unto the Lord,
Let us make a joyful noise to the rock of our salvation.
Let us come before his presence with thanksgiving,
Let us make a joyful noise unto him with psalms.
Enter into his gates with thanksgiving,
And into his courts with praise.
Give thanks unto him, and bless his name.
For the Lord is good; his mercy endureth forever;
And his faithfulness unto all generations. Amen.

HOLY, HOLY, HOLY, LORD GOD ALMIGHTY!

NICÆA. 11s, 12s & 10s.

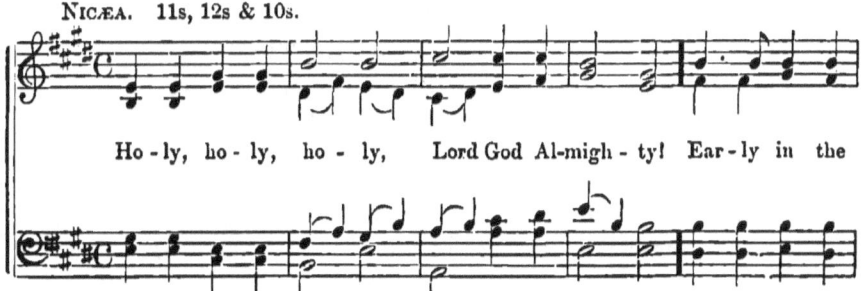

Ho - ly, ho - ly, ho - ly, Lord God Al-migh - ty! Ear - ly in the

morn-ing our song shall rise to thee; Ho-ly, ho-ly, ho-ly, mer-ci-ful and might-y, God in three per-sons, blessed Trin-i-ty!

Holy, holy, holy! all the saints adore Thee,
    Casting down their golden crowns around the glassy sea;
Cherubim and seraphim falling down before Thee
    Which wert and art and evermore shalt be.

Holy, holy, holy! though the darkness hide Thee,
    Though the eye of sinful man Thy glory may not see;
Only Thou art holy; there is none beside Thee,
    Perfect in power, in love and purity.

Holy, holy, holy! Lord God Almighty!
    All Thy works shall praise Thy name, in earth and sky and sea;
Holy, holy, holy! merciful and mighty,
    God in three persons, blessed Trinity!

M. If we say that we have no sin, we deceive ourselves, and the truth is not in us. If we confess our sins, he is faithful and righteous to forgive us our sins, and to cleanse us from all unrighteousness.

Confession. (Psalm LI.)

Have mercy upon me, O God, according to thy lovingkindness:
 According to the multitude of thy tender mercies blot out my transgressions.
Wash me thoroughly from mine iniquity,
 And cleanse me from my sin.
For I acknowledge my transgressions:
 And my sin is ever before me.
Against thee, thee only, have I sinned,
And done that which is evil in thy sight:
 That thou mayest be justified when thou speakest,
 And be clear when thou judgest.
Behold, I was shapen in iniquity;
And in sin did my mother conceive me.
 Behold, thou desirest truth in the inward parts:
 And in the hidden part thou shalt make me to know wisdom.
Purge me with hyssop, and I shall be clean:
 Wash me, and I shall be whiter than snow.
Make me to hear joy and gladness;
That the bones which thou hast broken may rejoice.
 Hide thy face from my sins,
 And blot out all mine iniquities.
Create in me a clean heart, O God;
 And renew a right spirit within me.
Cast me not away from thy presence;
 And take not thy holy spirit from me.
Restore unto me the joy of thy salvation:
 And uphold me with a free spirit.
Then will I teach transgressors thy ways;
And sinners shall be converted unto thee.
 Deliver me from bloodguiltiness, O God, thou God of my salvation;
 And my tongue shall sing aloud of thy righteousness.
O Lord, open thou my lips;
 And my mouth shall shew forth thy praise.
For thou delightest not in sacrifice; else would I give it:
 Thou hast no pleasure in burnt offering.
The sacrifices of God are a broken spirit:
 A broken and a contrite heart, O God, thou wilt not despise.

DE PROFUNDIS.

1 Out of the | depths ‖ Have I cried unto thee, O | Lord! ‖
2 Lord, hear my | voice: ‖ Let thine ears be attentive to the voice of my suppli- | cations. ‖
3 If thou, Lord, shouldst mark in- | iquities. ‖ O Lord! who shall | stand? ‖
4 But there is forgiveness with | thee, ‖ That thou mayest be | feared. ‖
5 I wait for the Lord, my soul doth | wait, ‖ And in his word do I | hope. ‖
6 My soul waiteth for the Lord more than they that watch for the | morning: ‖ I say, more than they that watch for the | morning. ‖
7 Let Israel hope in the | Lord; ‖ For with the Lord there is mercy, and with him is plenteous re- | demption. ‖
8 And he shall redeem | Israel ‖ From all his in- | iquities. ‖

A - men.

The Beatitudes. (*In unison.*) (MATT. 5: 3-12.)

Blessed are the poor in spirit: for theirs is the kingdom of heaven.
Blessed are they that mourn: for they shall be comforted.
Blessed are the meek: for they shall inherit the earth.
Blessed are they that hunger and thirst after righteousness: for they shall be filled.
Blessed are the merciful: for they shall obtain mercy.
Blessed are the pure in heart: for they shall see God.
Blessed are the peacemakers: for they shall be called sons of God.

Blessed are they that have been persecuted for righteousness' sake: for theirs is the kingdom of heaven. Blessed are ye when men shall reproach you, and persecute you, and say all manner of evil against you falsely, for my sake. Rejoice, and be exceeding glad: for great is your reward in heaven: for so persecuted they the prophets which were before you.

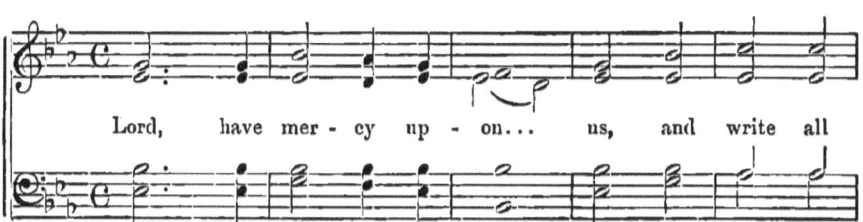

Lord, have mer-cy up-on... us, and write all

these thy words in our hearts, we beseech thee.

Praise. (Psalm CIII.)

Bless the Lord, O my soul;
    And all that is within me, bless his holy name.
Bless the Lord, O my soul,
    And forget not all his benefits:
Who forgiveth all thine iniquities;
    Who healeth all thy diseases;
Who redeemeth thy life from destruction;
    Who crowneth thee with lovingkindness and tender mercies:
Who satisfieth thy mouth with good things;
    So that thy youth is renewed like the eagle.

The Lord executeth righteous acts,
    And judgements for all that are oppressed.
He made known his ways unto Moses,
    His doings unto the children of Israel.
The Lord is full of compassion and gracious,
Slow to anger, and plenteous in mercy.
    He will not always chide;
    Neither will he keep his anger for ever.
He hath not dealt with us after our sins,
    Nor rewarded us after our iniquities.
For as the heaven is high above the earth,
So great is his mercy toward them that fear him.
    As far as the east is from the west,
    So far hath he removed our transgressions from us.
Like as a father pitieth his children,
    So the Lord pitieth them that fear him.
For he knoweth our frame ;
    He remembereth that we are dust.
As for man, his days are as grass ;
As a flower of the field, so he flourisheth.
    For the wind passeth over it, and it is gone;
    And the place thereof shall know it no more.
But the mercy of the Lord is from everlasting to everlasting upon them that fear him,
    And his righteousness unto children's children;
To such as keep his covenant,
And to those that remember his precepts to do them.
    The Lord hath established his throne in the heavens;
    And his kingdom ruleth over all.
Bless the Lord, ye angels of his:
    Ye mighty in strength, that fulfil his word,
    Hearkening unto the voice of his word.
Bless the Lord, all ye his hosts ;
    Ye ministers of his, that do his pleasure.
Bless the Lord, all ye his works,
In all places of his dominion :
    Bless the Lord, O my soul.

GLORIA PATRI.

Glory be to the Father, and | to the | Son,
And | to the | Holy | Ghost;
As it was in the beginning, is now, and | ever | shall be,
World with- | out end. | A-— | men.

Prayer.   (By the Minister.)

Scripture Lesson.

Anthem.

Address or Sermon.

Prayer.   (By the Minister and the People.)   (PSALM CXLIII.)

Hear my prayer, O Lord ; give ear to my supplications:
 In thy faithfulness answer me, and in thy righteousness.
And enter not into judgement with thy servant;
For in thy sight shall no man living be justified.
 I remember the days of old ;
 I meditate on all thy doings:
I muse on the work of thy hands.
I spread forth my hands unto thee :
 My soul thirsteth after thee, as a weary land.
Make haste to answer me, O Lord ; my spirit faileth:
 Hide not thy face from me ;
 Lest I become like them that go down into the pit.

Cause me to hear thy lovingkindness in the morning;
For in thee do I trust:
>Cause me to know the way wherein I should walk;
>For I lift up my soul unto thee.

Deliver me, O Lord, from mine enemies:
I flee unto thee to hide me.
>Teach me to do thy will; for thou art my God:
>Thy spirit is good; lead me in the land of uprightness.

Quicken me, O Lord, for thy name's sake:
In thy righteousness bring my soul out of trouble.

M. O Lord, save thy people, and bless thine heritage.

P. Gov-ern them, and lift them up for-ev-er.

M. Day by day we magnify Thee.

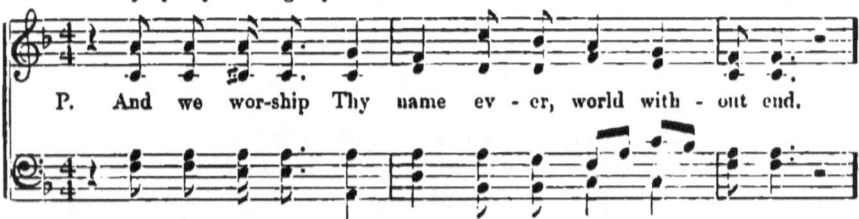

P. And we wor-ship Thy name ev-er, world with-out end.

M. Vouchsafe, O Lord, to keep us this day without sin.

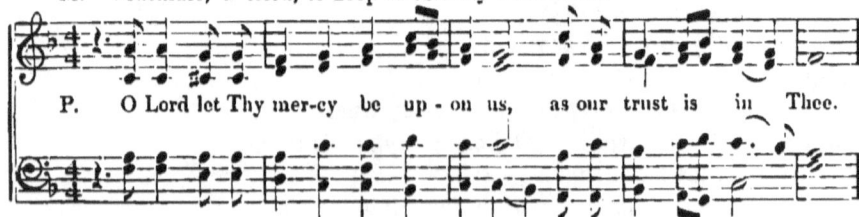

P. O Lord let Thy mer-cy be up-on us, as our trust is in Thee.

VESPER SERVICE.

ABIDE WITH ME!

Swift to its close ebbs out life's little day;
Earth's joys grow dim; its glories pass away;
Change and decay in all around I see;
O Thou, who changest not, abide with me!

Not a brief glance I beg, a passing word;
But, as Thou dwell'st with Thy disciples, Lord,
Familiar, condescending, patient, free,
Come, not to sojourn, but abide, with me!

Come not in terrors, as the King of kings;
But kind and good, with healing in Thy wings;
Tears for all woes, a heart for every plea;
Come, Friend of sinners, and thus 'bide with me.

Thou on my head in early years didst smile,
And though rebellious and perverse meanwhile,
Thou hast not left me, oft as I left Thee:
On to the close, O Lord, abide with me!

I need Thy presence every passing hour;
What but Thy grace can foil the Tempter's power?
Who like Thyself my guide and stay can be?
Through cloud and sunshine, O abide with me!

MINISTER. — Let us pray.

Almighty God, who seest that we have no power of ourselves to help ourselves; keep us both outwardly in our bodies, and inwardly in our souls; that we may be defended from all adversities which may happen to the body, and from all evil thoughts which may assault and hurt the soul; through Jesus Christ our Lord. Amen.

[OR THIS.]

O Almighty Lord, vouchsafe, we beseech thee, to direct, sanctify, and govern, both our hearts and bodies, in the ways of the laws, and in the works of thy commandments; that, through thy most mighty protection, both here and ever, we may be preserved in body and soul; through our Lord and Saviour, Jesus Christ. Amen.

[OR THIS.]

Direct us, O Lord, in all our doings, with thy most gracious favor, and further us with thy continual help; that in all our works begun, continued, and ended in thee, we may glorify thy holy name, and finally, by thy mercy obtain eternal life: through Jesus Christ our Lord. Amen.

THE DAY, O LORD.

[The Choir.]

The day, O Lord! is spent; Abide with us, and rest;
Our hearts' desires are fully bent On making Thee our guest.

We have not reached that land,
That happy land, as yet,
Where holy angels round Thee stand
Whose sun can never set.

Our sun is sinking now;
Our day is almost o'er;
O Sun of righteousness! do Thou
Shine on us evermore.

The Benediction.

The grace of our Lord Jesus Christ, the love of God, and the communion of the Holy Spirit be with you all.

Response.

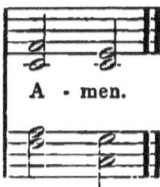

A - men.

VESPER SERVICE.

No. 3.

MINISTER. — It is very meet, right, and our bounden duty, that we should at all times, and in all places, give thanks unto thee, O Lord, Holy Father, Almighty, Everlasting God.

PEOPLE. — Therefore with angels and archangels, and with all the company of heaven, we laud and magnify thy glorious name; evermore praising thee and saying, Holy, holy, holy, Lord God of hosts, heaven and earth are full of thy glory. Glory be to thee, O Lord most high. Amen.

MINISTER. — Let us pray.

Direct us, O Lord, in all our doings, with thy most gracious favor, and further us with thy continual help, that in all our works begun, continued, and ended in thee, we may glorify thy holy name, and finally, by thy mercy, obtain eternal life, through Jesus Christ our Lord. Amen.

[OR THIS.]

O God, Holy Ghost, sanctifier of the faithful, visit, we pray thee, this congregation with thy love and favor: enlighten their minds more and more with the light of the everlasting gospel; graft in their hearts a love of the truth; increase in them true religion: nourish them with all goodness; and of thy great mercy keep them in the same, O blessed Spirit, whom, with the Father and the Son together, we worship and glorify as one God, world without end. Amen.

THE HOLY TRINITY.

The Rt. Rev. RICHARD MANT, D.D., Bp. of
Down and Connor (1776—1848), 1837.

The Rev. JOHN BACCHUS DYKES,
Mus. Doc. (1823—1876).

Round the Lord in glo-ry seat-ed, Cher-u-bim and Ser-a-phim
Filled His tem-ple and re-peat-ed, Each to each, th'alter-nate hymn: A-men.

"Lord, thy glory fills the heaven.
   Earth is with its fulness stored;
Unto thee be glory given,
   Holy! Holy! Holy! Lord!"

Heaven is still with glory ringing,
   Earth takes up the angels' cry,
"Holy! Holy! Holy! singing,
   Lord of hosts, the Lord most high!"

With his seraph-train before him,
   With his holy Church below,
Thus conspire we to adore him,
   Bid we thus our anthem flow:

"Lord, thy glory fills the heaven,
   Earth is with its fulness stored;
Unto thee be glory given,
   Holy! Holy! Holy! Lord!" Amen.

MINISTER. — Seek ye the Lord while he may be found, call ye upon him while he is near.

Let the wicked forsake his way, and the unrighteous man his thoughts: and let him return unto the Lord, and he will have mercy upon him; and to our God, for he will abundantly pardon.

Thus saith the high and lofty One, that inhabiteth eternity, whose name is Holy: I dwell in the high and holy place, with him also that is of a contrite and humble spirit, to revive the spirit of the humble, and to revive the heart of the contrite.

The Confession.

ALL. — Almighty and most merciful Father; We have erred and strayed from thy ways like lost sheep. We have followed too much the devices and desires of our own hearts. We have offended against thy holy laws. We have left undone those things which we ought to have done; and we have done those things which we ought not to have done; and there is no health in us. But thou, O Lord, have mercy upon us, miserable offenders. Spare thou those, O Lord, who confess their faults. Restore thou those who are penitent; according to thy promises declared unto mankind in Christ Jesus our Lord. And grant, O most merciful Father, for his sake: that we may hereafter live a godly, righteous, and sober life, to the glory of thy holy name. Amen.

The Lord's Prayer. *(In unison.)*

Our Father which art in heaven, Hallowed be thy name. Thy kingdom come. Thy will be done in earth, as it is in heaven. Give us this day our daily bread. And forgive us our debts, as we forgive our debtors. And lead us not into temptation, but deliver us from evil: For thine is the kingdom, and the power, and the glory, for ever. Amen.

MINISTER. — Our Lord Jesus Christ saith:

Ye are the light of the world. Let your light so shine before men, that they may see your good works, and glorify your Father which is in heaven.

Love your enemies, and pray for them that persecute you; that ye may be the sons of your Father which is in heaven.

When thou doest alms, let not thy left hand know what thy right hand doeth: that thy alms may be in secret.

When thou prayest, enter into thine inner chamber, and having shut thy door, pray to thy Father which is in secret.

Lay up not for yourselves treasures upon the earth, where moth and rust doth consume, and where thieves break through and steal: but lay up for yourselves treasures in heaven, where neither moth nor rust doth consume, and where thieves do not break through nor steal: for where thy treasure is, there will thy heart be also.

Be not anxious for your life, what ye shall eat, or what ye shall drink, nor yet for your body, what ye shall put on.

For your heavenly Father knoweth that ye have need of all these things.

But seek ye first his kingdom, and his righteousness; and all these things shall be added unto you.

Judge not, that ye be not judged.

All things, therefore, whatsoever ye would that men should do unto you, even so do ye also unto them: for this is the law and the prophets.

Not every one that saith unto me, Lord, Lord, shall enter into the kingdom of heaven; but he that doeth the will of my Father which is in heaven.

Lord, have mer-cy up-on us, ... and write all these thy laws in our hearts, we be-seech thee.

PSALM XXXIII.

Rejoice in the Lord, O ye righteous:
   Praise is comely for the upright.
Give thanks unto the Lord with harp:
   Sing praises unto him with the psaltery of ten strings.
Sing unto him a new song;
   Play skilfully with a loud noise.
For the word of the Lord is right;
   And all his work is done in faithfulness.
He loveth righteousness and judgement:
   The earth is full of the lovingkindness of the Lord.
By the word of the Lord were the heavens made;
   And all the host of them by the breath of his mouth.
He gathereth the waters of the sea together as an heap:
   He layeth up the deeps in storehouses.
Let all the earth fear the Lord:
   Let all the inhabitants of the world stand in awe of him.
For he spake, and it was done;
   He commanded, and it stood fast.
The Lord bringeth the counsel of the nations to nought:
   He maketh the thoughts of the peoples to be of none effect.
The counsel of the Lord standeth fast for ever,
   The thoughts of his heart to all generations.
Blessed is the nation whose God is the Lord;
   The people whom he hath chosen for his own inheritance.
The Lord looketh from heaven;
He beholdeth all the sons of men;
   From the place of his habitation he looketh forth
   Upon all the inhabitants of the earth;
He that fashioneth the hearts of them all,
That considereth all their works.
   There is no king saved by the multitude of an host.
A mighty man is not delivered by great strength.
   An horse is a vain thing for safety:
   Neither shall he deliver any by his great power.

Behold, the eye of the Lord is upon them that fear him.
Upon them that hope in his mercy;
  To deliver their soul from death,
  And to keep them alive in famine.
Our soul hath waited for the Lord:
  He is our help and our shield,
For our heart shall rejoice in him,
  Because we have trusted in his holy name.
Let thy mercy, O Lord, be upon us.
  According as we have hoped in thee.

GLORIA PATRI.

Farrant.

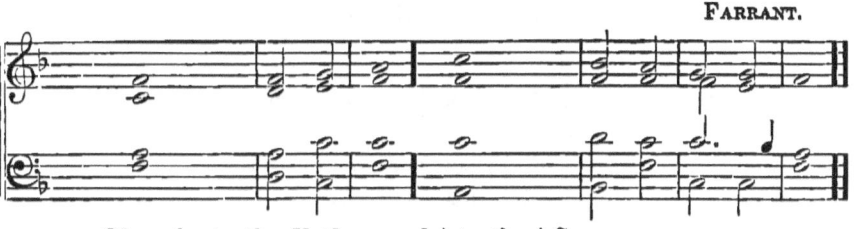

Glory be to the Father, and | to the | Son,
  And | to the | Holy Ghost;
As it was in the beginning, is now, and | ever | shall be,
  World | without | end. A | men.

Scripture Lesson.

Anthem.

Prayer. (By the Minister.)

STILL, STILL WITH THEE!

H. B. Stowe. Mendelssohn.

Still, still with thee when pur-ple morn-ing break-eth, When the bird

wak-eth, and the sha-dows flee; Fair-er than morn-ing, love-lier than the day-light, Dawns the sweet con-sciousness I am with thee!

Still, still with thee! as to each new-born morning
A fresh and solemn splendor still is given,
So does this blessed consciousness awaking,
Breath, each day, nearness unto thee and heaven.

When sinks the soul, subdued by toil, to slumber,
Its closing eye looks up to thee in prayer.
Sweet the repose beneath thy wings o'ershading,
But sweeter still, to wake and find thee there.

So shall it be at last, in that bright morning,
When the soul waketh, and life's shadows flee;
Oh, in that hour, fairer than daylight dawning,
Shall rise the glorious thought — I am with thee.

Address or Sermon.

MINISTER. — Let us pray.

PSALM XLV.

Hear my cry, O God:
Attend unto my prayer.
 From the end of the earth will I call unto thee, when my heart is overwhelmed:

Lead me to the rock that is higher than I.
> For thou hast been a refuge for me,
> A strong tower from the enemy.

I will dwell in thy tabernacle for ever:
> I will take refuge in the covert of thy wings.

For thou, O God, hast heard my vows:
> Thou hast given me the heritage of those that fear thy name.

My soul waiteth only upon God:
From him cometh my salvation.
> He only is my rock and my salvation:
> He is my high tower; I shall not be greatly moved.

My soul, wait thou only upon God;
> For my expectation is from him.

He only is my rock and my salvation:
> He is my high tower; I shall not be moved.

With God is my salvation and my glory:
> The rock of my strength, and my refuge, is in God.

Trust in him at all times, ye people;
Pour out your heart before him:
> God is a refuge for us.

God hath spoken once,
Twice have I heard this;
That power belongeth unto God:
> Also unto thee, O Lord, belongeth mercy:
> For thou renderest to every man according to his work.

O God, thou art my God; early will I seek thee:
> My soul thirsteth for thee, my flesh longeth for thee,
> In a dry and weary land, where no water is.

So have I looked upon thee in the sanctuary,
To see thy power and thy glory.
> For thy lovingkindness is better than life;
> My lips shall praise thee.

So will I bless thee while I live:
> I will lift up my hands in thy name.

My soul shall be satisfied as with marrow and fatness;
And my mouth shall praise thee with joyful lips;
> When I remember thee upon my bed,
> And meditate on thee in the night watches.

For thou hast been my help,
And in the shadow of thy wings will I rejoice.
　My soul followeth hard after thee:
　Thy right hand upholdeth me.

(Then this or the following hymn may be sung. When this hymn is sung, the next will be omitted.)

BREAK THOU THE BREAD OF LIFE.

Mary A. Lathbury.　　　　　　Wm. E. Sherwin. 1877, by per.

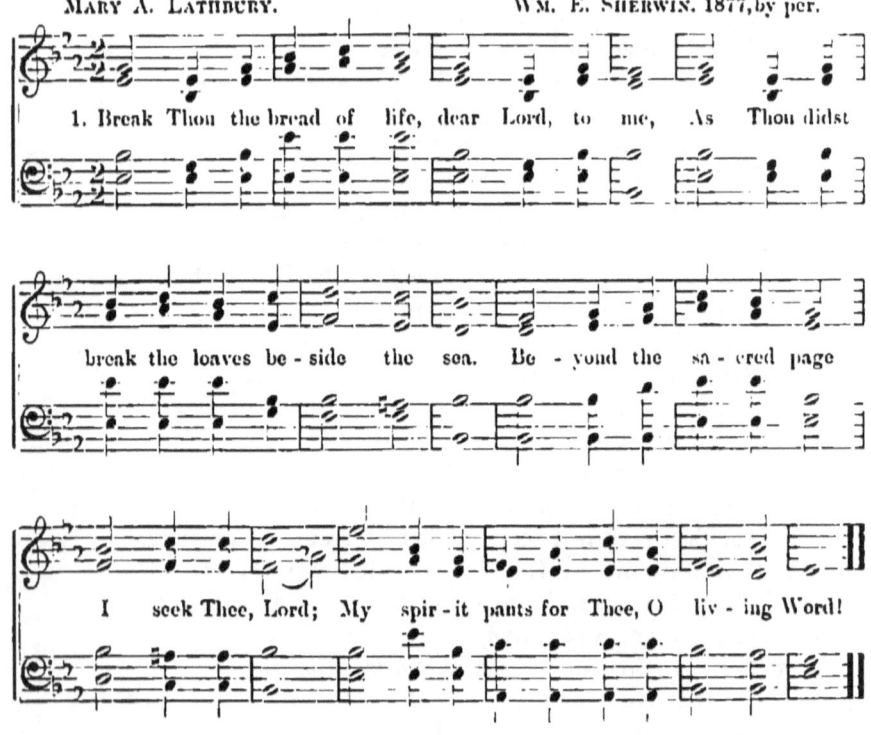

1. Break Thou the bread of life, dear Lord, to me, As Thou didst break the loaves be-side the sea. Be-yond the sa-cred page I seek Thee, Lord; My spir-it pants for Thee, O liv-ing Word!

　　Bless Thou the truth, dear Lord,
　　　　To me, to me,
　　As Thou didst bless the bread by Galilee;
　　Then shall all bondage cease,
　　　　All fetters fall,
　　And I shall find my peace,
　　　　My All in All!

HUSHED WAS THE EVENING HYMN!

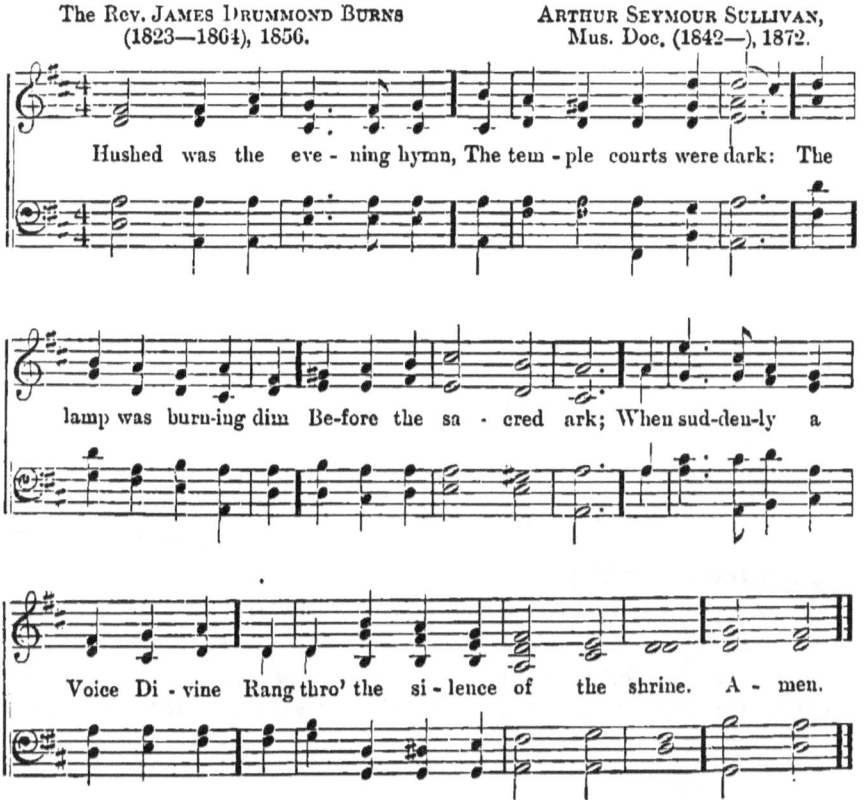

The Rev. James Drummond Burns (1823—1864), 1856.
Arthur Seymour Sullivan, Mus. Doc. (1842—), 1872.

The old man, meek and mild.
The priest of Israel, slept;
His watch the temple-child,
The little Levite, kept;
And what from Eli's sense was sealed,
The Lord to Hannah's son revealed.

Oh! give me Samuel's ear,
  The open ear, O Lord,
Alive and quick to hear
  Each whisper of thy Word;
Like him to answer at thy call,
And to obey thee first of all.

Oh! give me Samuel's heart,
  A lowly heart, that waits
Where in thy house thou art,
  Or watches at thy gates
By day and night; a heart that still
Moves at the breathing of thy will.

Oh! give me Samuel's mind,
  A sweet, unmurmuring faith,
Obedient and resigned
  To thee in life and death;
That I may read with childlike eyes
Truths that are hidden from the wise.
         Amen.

MINISTER. — Let us pray.

O Lord, who never failest to help and govern those whom thou dost bring up in thy steadfast fear and love; Keep us, we beseech thee, under the protection of thy good providence, and make us to have a perpetual fear and love of thy holy name; through Jesus Christ our Lord.

PEOPLE. — Amen.

[OR THIS.]

Almighty God, who hast promised to hear the petitions of those who ask in thy Son's name; We beseech thee mercifully to incline thine ears to us who have now made our prayers and supplications unto thee; and grant, that those things which we have faithfully asked according to thy will, may effectually be obtained, to the relief of our necessity, and the setting forth of thy glory; through Jesus Christ our Lord. Amen.

AS NOW THE SUN'S DECLINING RAYS!

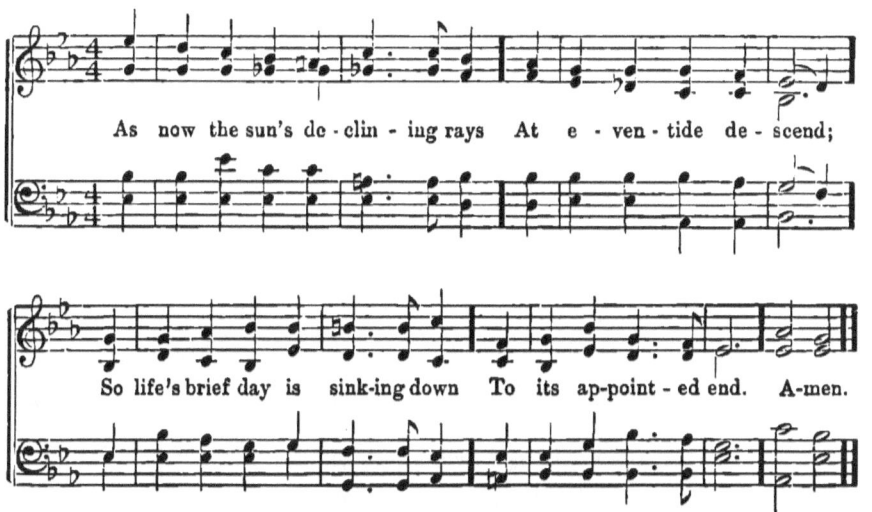

As now the sun's de-clin-ing rays At e-ven-tide de-scend;
So life's brief day is sink-ing down To its ap-point-ed end. A-men.

Lord, on the cross thine arms were stretched
To draw thy people nigh;
O grant us then that cross to love,
And in those arms to die.

Benediction.

The grace of our Lord Jesus Christ, and the love of God, and the fellowship of the Holy Ghost, be with us all evermore.

Response.

A - men.

Vesper Service.

No. 4.

MINISTER. — Praise waiteth for thee, O God, in Zion:
And unto thee shall the vow be performed.
O Thou that hearest prayer,
Unto thee shall all flesh come.

Oh, that men would praise the Lord for his goodness,
And for his wonderful works to the children of men!
And let them offer the sacrifices of thanksgiving,
And declare his works with singing.

Behold, bless ye the Lord, all ye servants of the Lord,
Which by night stand in the house of the Lord.
Lift your hands to the sanctuary,
And bless ye the Lord.

[CHOIR.]

Glo - ry be to Thee, O Lord, Most High!

HARK! HARK, MY SOUL!

Sing-ing to wel-come the pilgrims, the pilgrims of the night! A-men.

  Onward we go, for still we hear them singing,
   "Come, weary souls, for Jesus bids you come!"
  And through the dark its echoes sweetly ringing,
   The music of the gospel leads us home.
    Angels of Jesus, etc.

  Far, far away, like bells at evening pealing,
   The voice of Jesus sounds o'er land and sea,
  And laden souls by thousands meekly stealing,
   Kind Shepherd, turn their weary steps to thee.
    Angels of Jesus, etc.

  Rest comes at length, though life be long and dreary,
   The day must dawn, and darksome night be past;
  Faith's journey ends in welcome to the weary,
   And heaven, the heart's true home, will come at last.
    Angels of Jesus, etc.

The Confession. *(In unison.)*

 Almighty God, Father of our Lord Jesus Christ, Maker of all things, Judge of all men; We acknowledge and bewail our manifold sins and wickedness, which we, from time to time, most grievously have committed, by thought, word, and deed, against thy Divine Majesty, provoking most justly thy wrath and indignation against us. We do earnestly repent, and are heartily sorry for these our misdoings; the remembrance of them is grievous unto us; the burden of them is intolerable. Have mercy upon us, have mercy upon us, most merciful Father; for thy Son our Lord Jesus Christ's sake, forgive us all that is past; and grant that we may ever hereafter serve and please thee in newness of life, to the honor and glory of thy name; through Jesus Christ our Lord. Amen.

The Lord's Prayer.

Our Father which art in heaven, Hallowed be thy name. Thy kingdom come. Thy will be done in earth, as it is in heaven. Give us this day our daily bread. And forgive us our debts, as we forgive our debtors. And lead us not into temptation, but deliver us from evil: For thine is the kingdom, and the power, and the glory, for ever. Amen.

The Creed.

MINISTER. — Lord, increase our faith.

ALL. — I believe in God the Father Almighty, Maker of heaven and earth; and in Jesus Christ, his only Son our Lord, who was conceived by the Holy Ghost, born of the Virgin Mary, suffered under Pontius Pilate, was crucified, dead, and buried; he descended into hell; the third day he rose again from the dead; he ascended into heaven, and sitteth on the right hand of God the Father Almighty; from thence he shall come to judge the quick and the dead. I believe in the Holy Ghost; the Holy Catholic Church; the communion of saints; the forgiveness of sins; the resurrection of the body, and the life everlasting. Amen.

1 HOLY, holy, holy, | Lord God Al- | mighty!
2 Which was, and | is, and | is to come.
3 Thou art worthy, O Lord! to receive glory and | honor and | power;
4 For thou hast created all things,
 And for thy pleasure they | are and | were cre- | ated.
5 Worthy is the Lamb | that was | slain,
6 To receive power, and riches, and wisdom,
 And strength, and | honor, and | glory, and blessing.
7 Blessing, and honor, and | glory, and | power,
8 Be unto him that sitteth upon the throne,
 And unto the | Lamb for | ever and | ever. Amen.

VESPER SERVICE. 41

MINISTER. — Hear the words of the Lord Jesus, how he said: —
Abide in me, and I in you. As the branch cannot bear fruit of itself, except it abide in the vine; so neither can ye, except ye abide in me. I am the vine, ye are the branches: he that abideth in me, and I in him, the same beareth much fruit: for apart from me ye can do nothing.

Herein is my Father glorified, that ye bear much fruit; and so shall ye be my disciples. Even as the Father hath loved me, I also have loved you: abide ye in my love. If ye keep my commandments, ye shall abide in my love; even as I have kept my Father's commandments, and abide in his love.

This is my commandment, that ye love one another, even as I have loved you.

Ye did not choose me, but I chose you, and appointed you, that ye should go and bear fruit, and that your fruit should abide.

LORD, HAVE MERCY UPON US!

WORSHIP.

The Lord is my light and my salvation; whom shall I fear?
The Lord is the strength of my life; of whom shall I be afraid?
When evil doers came upon me to eat up my flesh,
Even mine adversaries and my foes, they stumbled and fell.

Though an host should encamp against me,
  My heart shall not fear:
Though war should rise against me,
  Even then will I be confident.
One thing have I asked of the Lord, that will I seek after;
  That I may dwell in the house of the Lord all the days of my life,
  To behold the beauty of the Lord, and to inquire in his temple.
For in the day of trouble he shall keep me secretly in his pavilion:
  In the covert of his tabernacle shall he hide me;
  He shall lift me up upon a rock.
And now shall mine head be lifted up above mine enemies round about me;
  And I will offer in his tabernacle sacrifices of joy;
  I will sing, yea, I will sing praises unto the Lord.
Hear, O Lord, when I cry with my voice:
  Have mercy also upon me, and answer me.
When thou saidst, Seek ye my face; my heart said unto thee,
Thy face, Lord, will I seek.

GLORIA PATRI!

Glory be to the Father, and............ to the Son, and to the Ho-ly Ghost;

As it was in the beginning, is now, and.. ev-er shall be, world without end. A-men.

Scripture Lesson.

Anthem. [By the Choir.]

VESPER SERVICE.

Prayer. [By the Pastor.]

[Then this or the following hymn may be sung.]

"O, taste and see that the Lord is good."

Rev. John Samuel Bewley Monsell, L.L.D. 1811—1875.   Joseph Barnby.

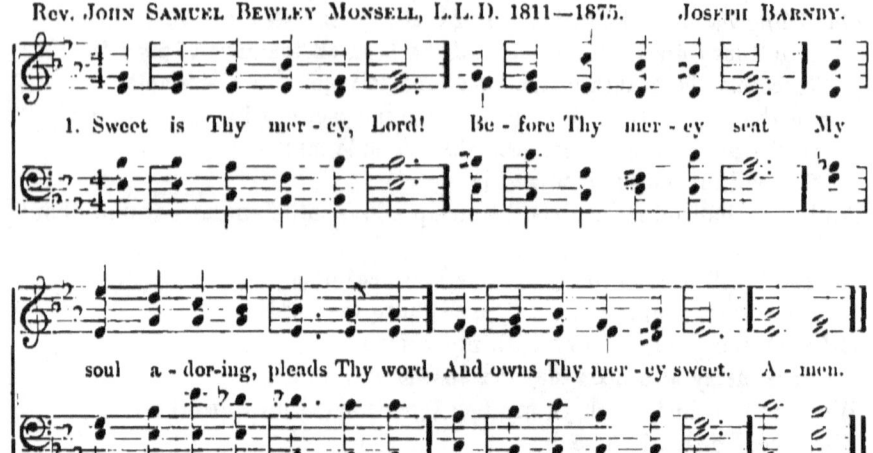

1. Sweet is Thy mer-cy, Lord! Be-fore Thy mer-cy seat My soul a-dor-ing, pleads Thy word, And owns Thy mer-cy sweet. A-men.

My need, and thy desires,
　Are all in Christ complete;
Thou hast the justice truth requires,
　And I thy mercy sweet.

Where'er thy name is blest,
　Where'er thy people meet,
There I delight in thee to rest,
　And find thy mercy sweet.

Light Thou my weary way,
　Place Thou my weary feet,
That while I stray on earth I may
　Still find thy mercy sweet.

Thus shall the heavenly host
　Hear all my songs repeat.
To Father, Son, and Holy Ghost,
　Thy joy, thy mercy sweet.　Amen.

44 VESPER SERVICE.

Hymn. JESUS, THOU JOY OF LOVING HEARTS!

Je-sus, thou joy of lov-ing hearts! Thou Fount of Life! Thou Light of men! From the best bliss that earth im-parts, We turn un-filled to thee a-gain. A-men.

Thy truth unchanged has ever stood;
  Thou savest those who on thee call;
To them that seek thee thou art good,
  To them that find thee, All in All.

We taste thee, O Thou Living Bread,
  And long to feast upon thee still;
We drink of thee, the Fountain Head,
  And thirst our souls from thee to fill.

Our restless spirits yearn for thee,
  Where'er our changeful lot is cast;
Glad when thy gracious smile we see.
  Blest when our faith can hold thee fast.

O Jesus, ever with us stay,
  Make all our moments calm and bright;
Chase the dark night of sin away, —
  Shed o'er the world thy holy light!

Sermon or Address.

WORSHIP.

I will lift up mine eyes unto the mountains:
From whence shall my help come?
    My help cometh from the Lord,
    Which made heaven and earth.
He will not suffer thy foot to be moved:
He that keepeth thee will not slumber.
    Behold, he that keepeth Israel
    Shall neither slumber nor sleep.
The Lord is thy keeper:
The Lord is thy shade upon thy right hand.
    The sun shall not smite thee by day,
    Nor the moon by night.
The Lord shall keep thee from all evil;
He shall keep thy soul.
    The Lord shall keep thy going out and thy coming in,
    From this time forth and for evermore.

Unto thee, O Lord, will I call;
My rock, be not thou deaf unto me:
    Lest, if thou be silent unto me,
    I become like them that go down into the pit.
Hear the voice of my supplications, when I cry unto thee,
When I lift up my hands toward thy holy oracle.
    Blessed be the Lord,
    Because he hath heard the voice of my supplications.
The Lord is my strength and my shield,
    My heart hath trusted in him, and I am helped:
Therefore my heart greatly rejoiceth;
And with my song will I praise him.
    The Lord is their strength,
    And he is a strong hold of salvation to his anointed.
Save thy people, and bless thine inheritance.
    Feed them also, and bear them up forever.

AT EVEN, ERE THE SUN WAS SET!

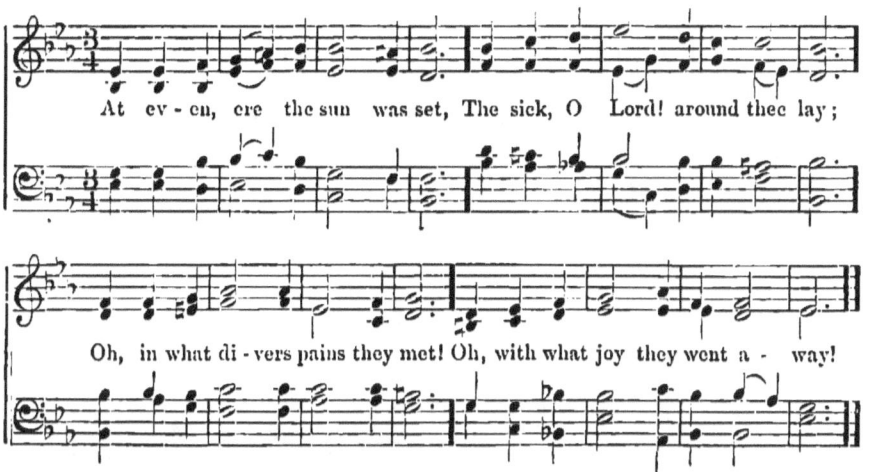

At ev-en, ere the sun was set, The sick, O Lord! around thee lay;
Oh, in what di-vers pains they met! Oh, with what joy they went a-way!

Once more 't is eventide, and we,
   Oppressed with various ills, draw near;
What if thy form we can not see?
   We know and feel that thou art here.

O Saviour Christ! our woes dispel,
   For some are sick and some are sad,
And some have never loved thee well,
   And some have lost the love they had;

And some have found the world is vain,
   Yet from the world they break not free,
And some have friends who give them pain,
   Yet have not sought a friend in thee.

O Saviour Christ! thou too art man;
   Thou hast been troubled, tempted, tried;
Thy kind but searching glance can scan
   The very wounds that shame would hide.

Thy touch has still its ancient power;
   No word from thee can fruitless fall;
Hear, in this solemn evening hour,
   And in thy mercy heal us all.

VESPER SERVICE.

MINISTER. — Almighty God, who hast given us grace at this time with one accord to make our common supplications unto thee; and dost promise that when two or three are gathered together in thy Name thou wilt grant their requests; Fulfil now, O Lord, the desires and petitions of thy servants, as may be most expedient for them; granting us in this world knowledge of thy truth, and in the world to come life everlasting. Amen.

(The Choir.) LORD, IN THIS THY MERCY'S DAY.

Lord, in this thy mer-cy's day, Ere it pass for aye a-way, On our knees we fall and pray.

A - men.

Holy Jesus, grant us tears,
Fill us with heart-searching fears
Ere that awful doom appears.

Lord, on us thy spirit pour,
Kneeling lowly at the door
Ere it close forevermore.

Grant us 'neath thy wings a place,
Lest we lose this day of grace
Ere we shall behold thy face.

Benediction.

The grace of the Lord Jesus Christ, and the love of God, and the communion of the Holy Ghost, be with you all. Amen.

VESPER SERVICE.

No. 5.

IT CAME UPON THE MIDNIGHT CLEAR!

Still through the cloven skies they come
   With peaceful wings unfurl'd;
And still their heavenly music floats
   O'er all the weary world:
Above its sad and lowly plains
   They bend on heavenly wing,
And ever o'er its Babel-sounds
   The blessed angels sing.

Yet with the woes of sin and strife
   The world has suffered long;
Beneath the angel-strain have rolled
   Two thousand years of wrong;
And men, at war with men, hear not
   The love-song which they bring:
Oh! hush the noise, ye men of strife,
   And hear the angels sing!

And ye, beneath life's crushing load,
   Whose forms are bending low,
Who toil along the climbing way
   With painful steps and slow;
Look now! for glad and golden hours
   Come swiftly on the wing:
Oh! rest beside the weary road,
   And hear the angels sing!

For lo! the days are hastening on,
   By prophet-bards foretold,
When with the ever-circling years
   Comes round the age of gold;
When Peace shall over all the earth
   Its ancient splendors fling,
And the whole world send back the song
   Which now the angels sing.   Amen.

Invocation.

MINISTER. — Arise, O Lord God, into thy resting place,
  PEOPLE. — Thou, and the ark of thy strength:
Let thy priests, O Lord God, be clothed with salvation,
  And let thy saints rejoice in goodness.
Behold, bless ye the Lord, all ye servants of the Lord, lift up your hands to the sanctuary, and bless ye the Lord.
  The Lord bless thee out of Zion; even he that made heaven and earth.
Praise ye the Lord, ye that stand in the house of the Lord.
  Sing praises unto his name; for it is pleasant.
Sing unto the Lord a new song, and his praise in the assembly of the saints.
  Let Israel rejoice in him that made him: let the children of Zion be joyful in their King.
I will pay my vows unto the Lord, in the courts of the Lord's house.
  Open to me the gates of righteousness: I will enter into them, I will give thanks unto the Lord.
This is the gate of the Lord; the righteous shall enter into it.
  I will give thanks unto thee, for thou hast answered me, and art become my salvation.

SONGS OF PRAISE THE ANGELS SANG.

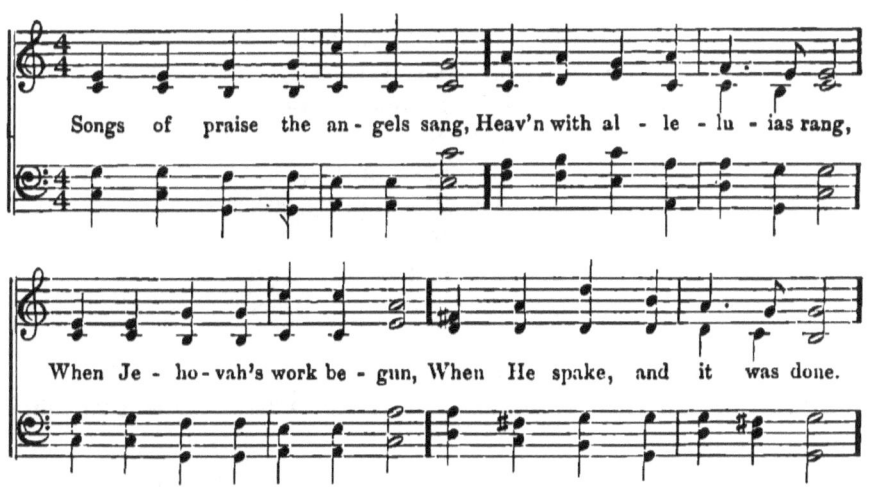

Songs of praise the an-gels sang, Heav'n with al-le-lu-ias rang,
When Je-ho-vah's work be-gun, When He spake, and it was done.

VESPER SERVICE.

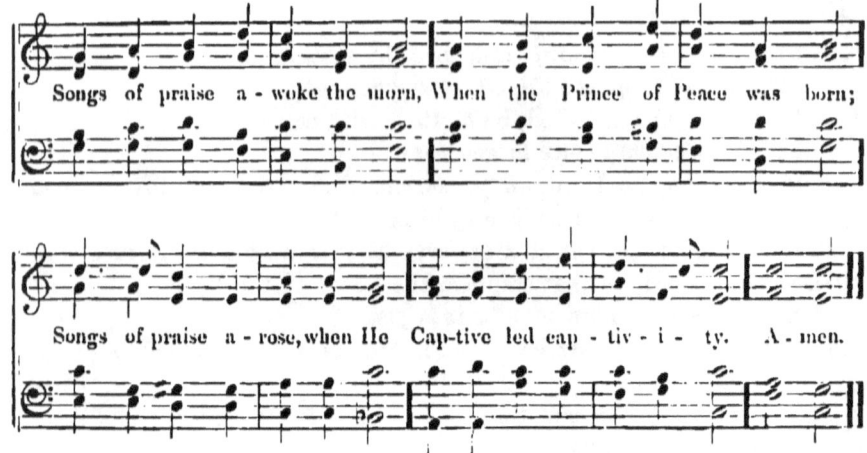

Songs of praise a-woke the morn, When the Prince of Peace was born;
Songs of praise a-rose, when He Cap-tive led cap-tiv-i-ty. A-men.

  Heaven and earth must pass away —
  Songs of praise shall crown that day;
  God will make new heavens, new earth —
  Songs of praise shall hail their birth.
  And shall man alone be dumb,
  Till that glorious kingdom come?
  No; the Church delights to raise
  Psalms and hymns and songs of praise.

  Saints below, with heart and voice,
  Still in songs of praise rejoice;
  Learning here, by faith and love,
  Songs of praise to sing above.
  Borne upon their latest breath,
  Songs of praise shall conquer death;
  Then, amidst eternal joy,
  Songs of praise their powers employ.
        Amen.

M. — Our Lord Jesus Christ saith: —
 The first of all the commandments is, Hear O Israel; the Lord our God is one Lord;

And thou shalt love the Lord thy God with all thy heart, and with all thy soul, and with all thy mind, and with all thy strength.

This is the first commandment. And the second is like, namely, this: Thou shalt love thy neighbour as thyself.

On these two commandments hang all the Law and the Prophets.

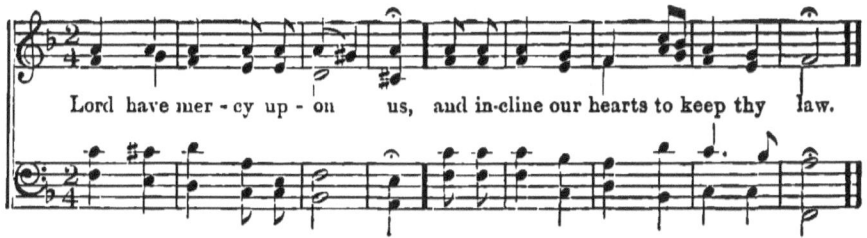

Lord have mer-cy up-on us, and in-cline our hearts to keep thy law.

The Apostles' Creed. [Recited in Unison.]

I believe in God the Father Almighty, Maker of heaven and earth: and in Jesus Christ his only Son our Lord, who was conceived by the Holy Ghost, born of the Virgin Mary, suffered under Pontius Pilate, was crucified, dead, and buried; he descended into hell; the third day he rose from the dead; he ascended into heaven, and sitteth on the right hand of God the Father Almighty; from thence he shall come to judge the quick and the dead. I believe in the Holy Ghost; the holy Catholic Church, the communion of saints; the forgiveness of sins; the resurrection of the body, and the life everlasting.

A - men.

M. — Let us pray. [Prayer by the Minister.]

Sermon or Address.

Thanksgiving.

I will extol thee, my God, O King;
    And I will bless thy name for ever and ever.
Every day will I bless thee;
    And I will praise thy name for ever and ever.

Great is the Lord, and highly to be praised,
And his greatness is unsearchable.
> One generation shall laud thy works to another,
> And shall declare thy mighty acts.

Of the glorious majesty of thine honour,
And of thy wondrous works, will I meditate.
> And men shall speak of the might of thy terrible acts;
> And I will declare thy greatness.

They shall utter the memory of thy great goodness,
And shall sing of thy righteousness.
> The Lord is gracious, and full of compassion;
> Slow to anger, and of great mercy.

The Lord is good to all;
And his tender mercies are over all his works.
> All thy works shall give thanks unto thee, O Lord;
> And thy saints shall bless thee.

They shall speak of the glory of thy kingdom,
And talk of thy power;
> To make known to the sons of men his mighty acts,
> And the glory of the majesty of his kingdom.

Thy kingdom is an everlasting kingdom,
And thy dominion endureth throughout all generations.
> The Lord upholdeth all that fall,
> And raiseth up all those that be bowed down.

The eyes of all wait upon thee;
And thou givest them their meat in due season.
> Thou openest thine hand,
> And satisfieth the desire of every living thing.

The Lord is righteous in all his ways,
And gracious in all his works.
> The Lord is nigh unto all them that call upon him,
> To all that call upon him in truth.

He will fulfil the desire of them that fear him;
He also will hear their cry, and will save them.
> The Lord preserveth all them that love him;
> But all the wicked will he destroy.

My mouth shall speak the praise of the Lord;
> And let all flesh bless his holy name for ever and ever.

GLORIA PATRI.

Glory be to the Father, and | to the | Son,
And | to the | Holy | Ghost;
As it was in the beginning, is now, and | ever | shall be,
World | without | end. A- | men.

Scripture Lesson.

Anthem.

Address or Sermon.

Supplication.   M. — Let us pray.   [Prayer by the Minister and People.]

Hear my prayer, O Lord; give ear to my supplications:
  In thy faithfulness answer me, and in thy righteousness.
And enter not into judgement with thy servant;
For in thy sight shall no man living be justified.
  I remember the days of old;
  I meditate on all thy doings:
I muse on the work of thy hands.
I spread forth my hands unto thee:
  My soul thirsteth after thee, as a weary land.
Make haste to answer me, O Lord; my spirit faileth:
  Hide not thy face from me;
  Lest I become like them that go down into the pit.
Cause me to hear thy lovingkindness in the morning;
For in thee do I trust:
  Cause me to know the way wherein I should walk;
  For I lift up my soul unto thee.

Deliver me, O Lord, from mine enemies:
I flee unto thee to hide me.
   Teach me to do thy will; for thou art my God:
   Thy spirit is good; lead me in the land of uprightness.
Quicken me, O Lord, for thy name's sake:
In thy righteousness bring my soul out of trouble.

COME, LORD, AND TARRY NOT.

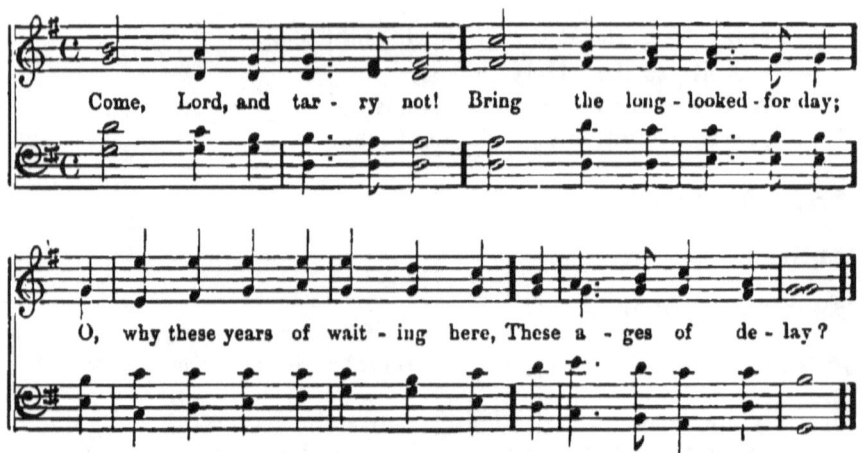

Come, for thy saints still wait;
  Daily ascends their sigh;
The Spirit and the Bride say, Come!
  Dost thou not hear the cry?

Come, for creation groans,
  Impatient of thy stay,
Worn out with these long years of ill,
  These ages of delay.

Come, and make all things new,
  Build up this ruined earth,
Restore our faded paradise,—
  Creation's second birth.

Come, and begin thy reign
  Of everlasting peace;
Come, take the kingdom to thyself,
  Great King of Righteousness!

VESPER SERVICE.

MINISTER. — Almighty God, who hast given us grace at this time with one accord to make our common supplications unto thee; and dost promise that when two or three are gathered together in thy name thou wilt grant their requests; Fulfil now, O Lord, the desires and petitions of thy servants, as may be most expedient for them; granting us in this world knowledge of thy truth, and in the world to come life everlasting. Amen.

JESUS, LORD AND MASTER.

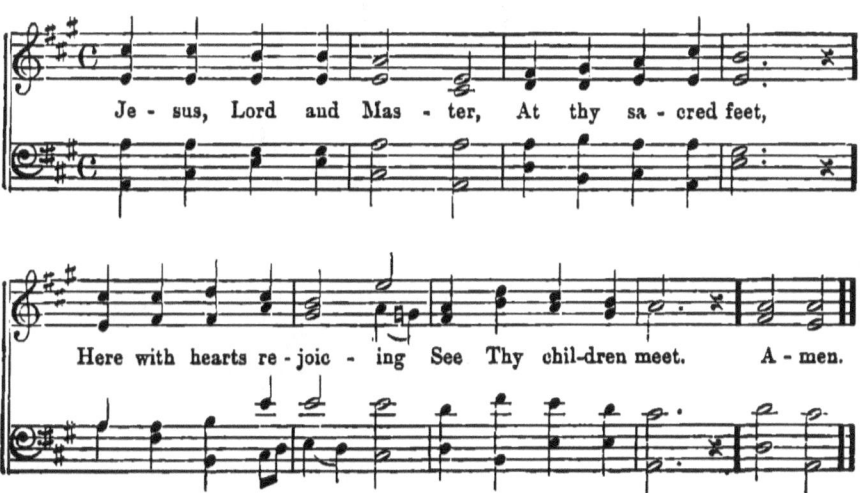

Je-sus, Lord and Mas-ter, At thy sa-cred feet, Here with hearts re-joic-ing See Thy chil-dren meet. A-men.

Often have we left thee,
Often gone astray;
Keep us, mighty Saviour,
In the narrow way.

All our days direct us
In the way we go;
Lead us on victorious
Over every foe:

Bid thine angels shield us
When the storm-clouds lower,
Pardon thou and save as
In the last dread hour.

The Benediction.

The grace of the Lord Jesus Christ, and the love of God, and the communion of the Holy Ghost, be with you all.

Response.

www.ingramcontent.com/pod-product-compliance
Lightning Source LLC
Chambersburg PA
CBHW031815220426
43662CB00007B/661